Images of Cornish Tin

Alan Stoyel and Peter Williams

Opposite page: Tin ingots at Wheal Jane. These represent the last stage in the processing of tin ore and also the final phase in the legacy of Cornish tin production. [BB98/21344/PW]

Images of Cornish Tin

Alan Stoyel and Peter Williams

CORNWALL LIBRARY

ENGLISH HERITAGE

Published by
Landmark Publishing Ltd,
Ashbourne Hall, Cokayne Ave
Ashbourne, Derbyshire DE6 1EJ England
Tel: (01335) 347349 Fax: (01335) 347303
e-mail: landmark@clara.net
web site: www.landmarkpublishing.co.uk

1st edition

ISBN 1 84306 020 5

© English Heritage 2001

British Library Cataloguing in Publication Data: a catalogue
record for this book is available from the British Library.

Printed by Centro Grafico Ambrosiano s.r.l

Design & reproduction by James Allsopp

Acknowledgements

Unless otherwise stated, the images have been taken by photographers from the Royal Commission on the Historical Monuments of England (RCHME) – Peter Williams, James O. Davies and Mike Hesketh-Roberts – and are © Crown copyright. NMR or © English Heritage (the RCHME merged with English Heritage in April 1999). Applications for the reproduction of images should be made to the National Monuments Record, National Monuments Record Centre, Great Western Village, Kemble Drive, Swindon SN2 2GZ. The National Monuments Record (NMR) negative number appears in square brackets at the end of the captions. Where relevant, in similar brackets, acknowledgement of other sources is given, together with a reference number, if required, for the image used.

We gratefully acknowledge permission from the following institutions and individuals to reproduce material which is either their copyright or held in their collections: B E C Howarth-Loomes: Page 20; Bridgeman Art Library/Royal Institution of Cornwall: Pages 43, 164 and 165; Bridgeman Art Library/Leeds Museums and Galleries: Page 81; Manchester City Art Galleries: Page 12; John Scott Martin: Pages 152 – 153; Victoria and Albert Picture Library: Pages 16, 28 and 99; and Phil Whiting: Page 15. Every effort has been made to trace copyright holders and we wish to apologise to any who may have been inadvertently omitted from the above list.

The authors are pleased to recognise the assistance of other colleagues in English Heritage who have helped in this publication. In particular, special mention should be made of: Roger Featherstone who took the aerial photographs at South Crofty and Wheal Jane, Keith Falconer who has helped in co-ordinating the final stage, Rachel Howard, Robin Taylor and Victoria Trainor from Academic and Specialist Publications, and Allan Brodie without whose support the project would never have begun.

A great debt of gratitude is owed to the men of South Crofty Mine and the treatment plant at Wheal Jane for the opportunity of recording scenes while the operations were still at work. In particular the authors would like to thank Bernard Ballard, Allen Buckley, Mike Hallewell and Steve Herbert for their help and patience. Acknowledgement is also given to Camborne School of Mines, Geevor Mine, The National Trust and the Trevithick Trust for giving generous access to their respective properties.

Thanks are due to the Royal Institution of Cornwall, and particularly to Roger Penhallurick, for assistance in photographing items and in supplying information about them.

Contents

Foreword

English Heritage has always sought to record and celebrate England's rich industrial heritage. The Cornish tin industry and its associated landscape have been in gradual decline over a long period of time, and this publication marks its effective passing as an active industry.

This book does not try to encompass the many facets of the work of English Heritage and its partners in the South-West, rather, it seeks to invoke the visual legacy of a culture dominated by the struggle to win tin from the ground. This selection, including many images available in the National Monuments Record (NMR), is that of the authors themselves and is essentially personal. They are well qualified to make that selection as Alan Stoyel, before joining the Royal Commission on the Historical Monuments of England (RCHME) as a field investigator, worked for many years as a mining geologist in Cornwall and abroad, while Peter Williams leads English Heritage's southern field photographic team. Between them, they have been responsible for taking and garnering a great many of the NMR images, although they would be the first to acknowledge the debt owed to the many friends and colleagues in assembling that collection.

We can be justly proud of our past efforts to record and preserve the remains of our industrial heritage, but we must constantly reaffirm their importance in the public eye. Illustrated books, such as this, devoted to part of that heritage, engage the interest of new audiences and serve to remind us of the importance of our industrial past.

Sir Neil Cossons, Chairman, English Heritage

Preface

This book is concerned with the tin-mining industry and the legacy of images which that uniquely distinctive industry has left. The justification for such a book is evident – for substantial periods over the last 4000 years the south-western peninsula of England was the principal source of tin in the western world. During the 18th and 19th centuries the Cornubian ore-field, which also covers west Devon, was, for a time, the world's greatest producer of tin and copper. The deep mining techniques developed in the area were exported to all corners of the mining world. The remains of that mining therefore have a significance far beyond Britain itself and this is being recognised by the nomination for World Heritage Site status of a cluster of seven areas which collectively represent the many facets of metal mining in the region.

The Cornish tin industry has attracted a considerable amount of attention both historically and, in more recent times, politically. Now, with the demise of the industry itself, its remains are attracting equally as much attention whether from planners, mining enthusiasts, historians, archaeologists or tourists. Over the last four decades much has been written about the subject and English Heritage (and its predecessors) in association with the Cornwall Archaeological Unit have endeavoured to identify, record and evaluate sites worthy of retention. Various recording programmes of aerial survey, archaeological field survey as on

Dartmoor and Bodmin Moor, and building and process recording as at Geevor, South Crofty and Wheal Jane, have all contributed greatly to our understanding of the industry. The component of English Heritage's Monuments Protection Programme devoted to Non-Metaliferrous Mining in the South-West has been informed by this work and is all the better for it. The work of the Cornwall Archaeological Unit on the ground has been spectacularly successful – inspired use of various funds for derelict land reclamation has resulted in a great many sites being properly consolidated rather than being cleared. Such effective advocacy and prioritisation of funding can only be achieved by thorough understanding of the archaeological resource built up over many years.

However, this book does not seek to reflect all this sterling work, rather it brings together a collection of images representing various expressions of the legacy of tin. The arrangement is loose and the choice is eclectic. There may be the occasional image that does not immediately appear relevant to the subject, but this is indicative of the wide ramifications and effects of the industry.

Over the last fifty years or so photographers of the Royal Commission on the Historical Monuments of England (RCHME), now merged with English Heritage, like many before them, have managed to capture some images of derelict mine buildings in south-west England. Photographs were taken because the structures were threatened with demolition or a significant change of character, or simply that they were such powerful and emotive features in the landscape. When the mine at Geevor finally closed in 1990 it was clear that a more concentrated effort to make a photographic record of what remained of the tin industry in Devon and Cornwall was needed.

During the last decade of the 20th century it was possible to make a 'snapshot' overview of what appears to be the last chapter of the tin industry in this corner of England. The final days of South Crofty Mine have been photographed, both underground and on the surface, by the RCHME as part of a process record of the mine shortly before its closure. The record of the extraction of the underground tin ore has been extended to include its subsequent raising to surface and processing to produce a tin concentrate for the smelter. Various other tin mines that were operating in Cornwall in recent years have been photographed after their demise, and an effort has been made to produce an archive of tin-related structures, artefacts and images.

The underground photographs that have been taken were an attempt to record the main stages in the mining of tin from only a few underground visits, but even these were necessarily an intrusion and a hindrance in the work of each miner involved. The underground environment is a hostile one. The darkness is total and has to be experienced to be appreciated. The temperature and humidity vary from one working-place to the next, but they are both generally high. Nearly everything in the mine is coated with an invasive dust, grit and mud, generally vivid orange-red. All gear has to be carried for long distances, not only horizontally, but also up and down constricted ladder-ways.

As the traditions of the mining industry lose their general familiarity the public image of tin mining is changing. This is demonstrated already by the way some mining sites and artefacts are advertised and presented. Fantasy is giving this tough and enduring industry a false romance and glamour that is not true to the generations that produced this aspect of Cornwall and Devon that we admire so much now. It is hoped that this book will, in a small way, increase general awareness of, and interest in, the tin industry and a respect for those who have been associated with it. The aim is to help foster a reverence for its monuments and landscapes, and its way of life and death. Much evidence still remains to be appreciated, but already the popular image of tin mining has degenerated more than that of the 'Cornish cream tea', and almost to the same level as the 'piskey'.

Alan Stoyel
Peter Williams
Keith Falconer

Introduction

From such derogatory terminology as tin sheds, tin cans, tin hats, tin lizzies and Tin Pan Alley it might be thought, quite wrongly, that tin is a metal of little value. It was the enabling of a small quantity of relatively precious tin metal to give a corrosion-free surface to a cheaply-produced iron or steel sheet that gave rise to these expressions. The tin plate industry was the greatest user of tin but, with the increased substitution of plastics and of aluminium, this market has largely disappeared. Traditionally tin has been of value in a number of well-known alloys: bronze which consists of copper and tin, pewter made of tin and lead, and solder also made of tin and lead.

Tin has been of great importance in the economies of Cornwall and Devon over many centuries. Its production has been directly associated with the price of the metal. The peak for tin mining was around 1870–2, since when there have been great fluctuations. After a period of almost thirty years of artificial international control, the Tin Council collapsed in 1985. Early that year the price of tin had touched £10,500 per ton but it dropped to £3,000 and has never recovered. South Crofty was the last tin mine in Europe to survive but it, too, closed on Friday, 6 March 1998.

The south-west of England is unique in the British Isles in possessing tin in significant amounts. Cornwall is the county that generally comes to mind in this connection, but Devon has also been a major producer of tin in the past. Despite its title, this book has included a number of images from east of the River Tamar; no tin has been mined in Britain further east or north than Dartmoor.

It must be remembered that tin is not the only metal that was mined in south-west England. Copper was of prime importance, but also significant were lead, zinc, silver, iron, tungsten, antimony, cobalt, nickel, uranium, arsenic and other minor elements. Of particular interest here is arsenic, commonly associated with tin mineralisation. This was once merely a noxious product of roasting the concentrated tin ore to drive off impurities. Later, tin-processing plants were designed with complex flues from which the salvage of the arsenic became a profitable operation. Arsenic production was important in Cornwall between about 1815 and 1950, with the peak from around 1860 until the end of Word War I. The main uses of arsenic were in insecticides and weedkillers, and as a decolouriser of glass, with later peaks of demand associated with fighting the cotton boll weevil and in the production of poison gas. The danger to health for workers associated with arsenic production can be imagined.

In Cornwall and Devon tin occurs in steeply-dipping mineral veins, or lodes as they are generally called, that cut through granite, or altered rocks associated with granite. The mining of tin and copper is inextricably linked in many of the mines. Some mines discovered deposits of tin, which could be economically exploited, at levels below where they had previously mined copper. The main ore of tin, cassiterite, is a hard and unreactive mineral, and the erosion of ground containing tin lodes has produced tin-bearing gravels in many of the valleys. Until about the last 250 years such gravels have probably produced the majority of the tin from this area.

Mining has had a significant effect on the landscape of parts of Cornwall and Devon. In some places the landscape itself has evolved from centuries of mining. The results range from the obvious to the subtle. Some mining structures have become part of the landscape, others intrude into it. Most can be understood with ease, a few are particularly thought-provoking. Each has significance and an undeniable appeal. Occasionally an association with tin is only revealed by the chance discovery of some structure or artefact, or by the sudden collapse of a previously unknown underground working.

Until the advent of the larger, deeper and more mechanised tin mines from the late 19th century onwards there was a more subtle blend of mining and agriculture. Mine buildings, such as dramatic engine houses, now dominate the landscape and act as forceful reminders of the underground quest for, and extraction of, tin ore. The bleak and relatively untouched landscapes of Dartmoor reveal some outstanding examples of many generations of tin-mining activity. Tin-streaming works dominate some of the valley bottoms and, here and there, have survived the ruins of a number of blowing houses, where tin was smelted in medieval times.

Despite the variety and interest of the mining landscape of Cornwall and Devon, and the drama of man battling with natural elemental forces, only a few sites have inspired artists to produce an artistic image of the tin industry.

For instance, a background such as Carn Brea with its castle and the Basset Monument, or the dramatic and exaggerated rim of a huge excavation was needed to add the necessary dramatic effect to make an engraving complete. Dolcoath Mine, seen on page 14, is unusual in that it shows only the industrial scene, although the site chosen was, after all, the greatest of the Cornish mines. Some of the most represented, and therefore best-known, examples of tin mines were situated on the north coast. This is partly because their dramatic locations on the cliffs have naturally been the focus of some interest. Mining accidents and disasters attracted public attention and, no doubt, these would have persuaded several engravers to journey to the far South-West. A plethora of late 19th- and early 20th-century children's books dwell on the dangerous and daring exploits of tin miners, often with sentimental and mawkish illustrations.

Some of the tin-mining images are thus true to life, others have been distorted to suit the purpose of the artist, eventually forming no more than an inspiration for a design. Few serious artists in watercolours or oils seem to have been attracted by mining scenes. This is surprising in view of the rich visual opportunities, and how close some of the operations associated with tin mining would have been to the artistic communities of St. Ives and Newlyn. Ownership of the mines by absent shareholders, coupled with the apparent lack of art sponsorship by the few prominent local families may also be reasons for the dearth of tin-related paintings – in striking contrast to the large number of artistic representations of the coal industry in other parts of the country. It appears that the other significant local industry, fishing, was the only one that was worthy of portrayal. Even in the post-war period prominent artists associated with Cornwall (Frost, Hepworth, Heron, Nicholson, etc) have produced little work relating to the tin industry. In the medium of photography the recording of mining scenes was more acceptable and a rich legacy of such images covering the last 150 years has survived.

Mine shafts came in a range of shapes and sizes and they constituted the vital connections with the underground world. Up came waste rock, ore and water, and down went timber and iron, tools and equipment. In recent times men were hoisted and lowered by cage, and compressed air was piped underground to drive machinery and to aid ventilation. Many early shafts were sunk at an angle, following the steeply-dipping mineral vein, or lode, downwards. These were frequently used for a specific purpose, such as pumping or hoisting, but modern shafts are large, vertical and generally deep as well as being multi-purpose. All shafts are dangerous, whether they are infilled, capped or open, fenced or unfenced, known or unknown.

Cornish tin mining was famed for the Cornish beam engine. These steam engines were primarily for pumping the water out of a mine, but they also hoisted the ore. Sometimes they powered stamps to crush the tin ore so that the tin-bearing mineral could be separated from the waste rock. That any beam engine still survives at a tin mine in Cornwall is due to the efforts of the Cornish Engines Preservation Society which was formed by a group of enthusiasts in 1935 and eventually succeeded in saving four engines in their engine houses. These are the whim, or winding engine, at Levant, Robinson's pumping engine at South Crofty, and Michell's whim and Taylor's pumping engine at East Pool. Later all the engines were handed over to The National Trust with an endowment fund.

When a mine closed in the past an engine would often be given a new lease of life at another mine, for example the engine now at Robinson's Shaft at South Crofty is at its fourth location. With the closure of tin mines in Cornwall in the 19th and the beginning of the 20th centuries many of the beam engines were broken up for scrap. Others were re-used in various industries in different parts of the country, and some were exported to foreign mines. The depression in tin mining coincided with expansion of the china-clay industry in Cornwall and a number of mine engines were moved and reinstalled to operate pumps in the St. Austell china-clay district.

As part of the local development of the high-pressure beam engine the Cornish boiler appeared, distinctive with its single flue, but few of these remain. For winding purposes the horizontal steam engine later became popular, but even fewer examples of these have survived *in situ*.

In recent times large electric hoists were installed at the mines, some having come second-hand from collieries. There were also small modern portable electric hoists that could be used underground or for temporary surface tasks. Such modern electric mine winders should not be overlooked completely. In the irony of the present climate, even though they are relatively rare in Cornwall, such machines are now more vulnerable than the old steam engines. Another vital element of the plant at a mine is the air compressor. Originally these were massive machines, powered by steam engines. Eventually such plants became electrically-powered and extremely compact.

Many people in Devon and Cornwall would be amazed by the amount of tunnelling that has taken place in the rocks beneath their feet. No fenced-off hole in the ground or derelict headframe can convey what life was really like below the surface. It has always been a strange and forbidden world and, with the closure of the last tin mine, access to this environment has all but disappeared. In South Crofty it has been calculated that the underground passages total over fifty miles. These horizontal tunnels were developed at various depths, traditionally measured in fathoms (units of 6 feet). What is perhaps more significant is the enormous volume of rock that has been removed between the various levels in the mine.

The processing of tin ore consists of the crushing or grinding of the rock and the separation of the tin mineral by various means, largely by gravity. In fact, the fine grain of the ore means that a perfect separation is impossible. The achievement of the highest grade of tin concentrate from a particular sample of tin ore with the minimum loss of the metal, and by the cheapest means possible, has always required a complex blend of science and skill. The treatment plant at Wheal Jane was the best of its kind in the world and included pieces of equipment that were 20th-century inventions. This contrasts dramatically with the traditional older methods including the world-famous Cornish stamps for crushing the ore.

The inherent danger associated with mining is attested by the numerous accidents that have been reported graphically in the past, but that have eventually relapsed into the blur of history. The discovery of a stone marking where a victim of an accident has been finally laid to rest indicates vividly something of the tragedy that such an event must have meant for the immediate family. Some families suffered losses that were reminiscent of wartime casualties. But this was not a test of loyalty in a call to arms for a finite military campaign; it was the real necessity of entering the dark, dirty and dangerous world of mining to enable the family to survive.

Methodism was well represented in the mining areas, and John Wesley had a strong following here. The many and varied chapels and meeting places are striking reminders of the religious fervour that typified the mining communities for more than 150 years from the mid-18th until the 20th century. Latterly men's institutes had become another common meeting place. As with the chapels, the institutes varied widely in scale, and both have suffered a similar decline in fortune. The Mining Exchange in Redruth is one indication of the wealth, or the dream of it, that accompanied dealing in the volatile world of mining stocks and shares. The benevolence and public spirit demonstrated by many of the mineral owners was fairly limited, even though some of them had accrued significant fortunes from tin mining. However the mining district did attract generous benefactors, such as J Passmore Edwards, and various inscriptions on public buildings throughout the area attest to some level of financial support being given to a number of mining communities.

The images selected here represent a variety of environments. Works of art and museum exhibits should have an assured future and will continue to be appreciated. The underground environment has virtually disappeared, most of it below the water that will have risen relentlessly, level by level. Of the remaining images many could still be recaptured, but careful comparison is likely to show that the subjects will have changed. Some changes have been dramatic, involving the demolition of buildings, others have been much more subtle. They are the effects of authorised and unauthorised human actions, together with the natural process of decay and vegetation growth. The result is the gradual, but relentless, erasing of some of the evidence of the tin industry in the landscape.

The Monuments Protection Programme of English Heritage has recognised the importance of the tin industry and some of the best sites have become Scheduled Monuments. This should prevent their active destruction but it is not a mechanism for the maintenance of the individual structures that are present. Most of the best of the built structures associated with the tin industry are classified as 'listed' buildings, which not only gives them protection but, hopefully, means that they will be kept in reasonable repair. There still survives much evidence that relates to the mining, concentrating or smelting of tin, from prehistoric to very recent times, that is outside any statutory protection. Individual sites, structures or relics may appear small or uninspiring. To some people they may be thought uninteresting, or even eyesores. To others such things engender pride and respect for what was achieved in the winning of tin in Cornwall and Devon.

The Landscape

The scenery of the tin-mining districts of Cornwall and Devon is very varied. Because tin mineralisation is associated with the granite masses of Dartmoor, Bodmin Moor, St. Austell Moor, Carnmenellis and Lands End, much of the landscape is open and somewhat bleak. In the 'moonscape' area to the north of St. Austell, which later became the major source of china clay, the effects of tin mining have been eclipsed by later earth-moving operations on a giant scale. Perhaps the best tin landscapes to survive are those of Dartmoor, due to their protection within a National Park, and of the Lands End peninsula, because of the relative remoteness of the sites. Elsewhere the dumps of waste rock have been removed for hardcore, for reprocessing for tin or some other product, as part of economic redevelopment or as a sometimes misguided 'cleaning up' operation on what has been classified as derelict land. In the same way the mine buildings and other structures have suffered from a relentless war of attrition.

The effects of tin mining on the landscape range from the transitory to the permanent. Scenes from historic engravings and paintings show the dramatic degree to which the industry has changed. In the interval between the taking of the photographs and the publication of this book a number of the recorded subjects have gone and those that remain are destined to change over the coming years.

A wintry view of Headland Warren Farm, south-west of North Bovey, Devon. In the foreground is some of the surface evidence of Headland Mine. The workings in the valley below the farm, and the trials on the hillside beyond, are associated with Vitifer Mine over the horizon. Vitifer was one of the better-known of the Dartmoor tin mines. [AA99/04977/PW]

A painting by James Clarke Hook (1819–1907) in the Manchester City Art Gallery, entitled 'From under the sea' showing Botallack Mine, St. Just in Penwith. Miners are seen in the 'gig' that conveyed them down the inclined shaft known as the Boscawen Diagonal Shaft. This shaft descended at an angle of $32^1/_2$ degrees and was started in 1858. The men would probably travel to the 165 fathom level, approximately 1,000 feet (302 m) vertically below this spot, as only ore and materials were drawn from levels below that. The 'gig' was chain-hauled by Pearce's Whim, a steam engine at The Crowns headland (*see* illustration on page 17).

The painting is romanticised, but beautifully detailed, and forms a rare image of a mining scene. Attesting to its accuracy, perched on the cliffs, in the background, is the shaft of Wheal Button. Despite the picture's present title it probably shows the miners about to descend into the mine because a bunch of fresh candles is visible hanging around the neck of one of them. In the foreground is an underground water flask, authentically dented, together with a large pasty. Exhibited at the Royal Academy in 1864, the patent sentimentality of the painting had probably been provoked by the breaking of the Boscawen Diagonal Shaft 'gig' chain on 18 April 1863 that resulted in the deaths of eight men and a boy. [Manchester City Art Galleries]

A Victorian illustration entitled 'A Tin Mine' showing a rather fanciful Carn Brea Mine. Of particular interest is the rectangular 'buddle' being used for separating the tin in the foreground. The artist was not very mechanically minded, as is demonstrated by the relationship between the wagon and its rails on the left-hand side. Carn Brea forms the background, topped by its monument (*see* illustration on page 44) and 'castle'.

A later engraving of Carn Brea Mine that appears as the frontispiece of *The Treasures of the Earth* by William Jones, published in 1868. It has clearly been copied from the original of the illustration *above*. This artist may have been concerned about the previous depiction of the wagon on its rails and has chosen the position of the left-hand margin with great subtlety. Carn Brea Mine closed in 1913.

An engraving of the remarkable tin mine at Carclaze Mine, near St. Austell. This was a mine of ancient foundation in which narrow tin lodes were scattered through highly altered granite over a wide area. The mine was developed mostly as a large open-cast pit and the waterwheels in the picture were part of a series of Cornish stamps to crush the hard part of the ore (Cornish stamps are dealt with more fully in Chapter 5). In the last quarter of the 19th century the workings were engulfed by major china-clay operations.

A well-known engraving of the great mine of Dolcoath that is thought to represent New Sump Shaft in about 1831. At this time the mine was celebrated for its copper production. It was to become just as famous later on for tin. Clearly artistic licence has been used, but some interesting features are depicted. A 'kibble' of ore has been drawn up the shaft to the surface by a powered rope from pulley-stands to the right. That this shaft was primarily for pumping is shown by the beam of the engine projecting over it. To the left is a capstan winch for raising and lowering materials in the shaft and the rope passes over the sheer-legs to enable long items, such as pump rods, to be accommodated. In the foreground are the 'bal maidens' (*see* illustration on page 158) who are cobbing the ore; breaking up the larger pieces and hand-picking the mineralised material for further treatment.

Although he originally came from Hull, Phil Whiting, who now lives in Cornwall, has been deeply influenced by the local landscapes, particularly by the mining industry. The abiding theme in his paintings is the physical relationship between mankind and the earth. His work, 'Wheal Jane', shows the geometrical arrangement of timbering that marks the mine shaft, thrusting downwards through the contrasting random irregularities of the Cornish rocks. This subterranean struggle between man and nature also contrasts with the serenity and light of the scene at the surface. [© Phil Whiting]

A depiction of a traditional Cornish engine house on a rocky coast by someone not normally associated with these familiar landscape features. It is a design for a tile by the famous potter Bernard Leach of St. Ives, now in the Victoria and Albert Museum collection. It probably dates from about 1929–30.
[V&A Picture Library: CT 19636]

Opposite top: The Crowns engine houses of the renowned Botallack Mine on the rugged north coast near St. Just in Penwith, viewed from the south. The left-hand engine house is a very old one and was used for pumping. The other once contained Pearce's Whim, the winding engine for the long, inclined Bocawen Diagonal Shaft, that went a considerable distance out to sea, illustrated on page 12. The mine closed in 1895. [AA98/10388/JOD]

Opposite below: An 1823 lithograph of Botallack Mine, published by John Tonkin in Penzance, now held in the museum at Geevor Mine. The accuracy of the mining elements in the picture is not as great as might be expected from the precise way in which they have been depicted. In addition, despite certain natural features in the landscape being recognisable, the whole scene has been exaggerated, as is shown by comparison with the illustration *opposite top*. [BB98/13704]

A plaque on the centrepiece of the boardroom silver at Geevor Mine, about a mile and a half (2.4 km) to the east of Botallack. This silver piece appears to be identical to the one that was made by Mappin and Webb for Richard Boyns of the bank at St. Just in 1880 and is illustrated in Cyril Noall's book, *Botallack*. The plaque shows elements that can only have been taken from the same view of Botallack Mine that has been the subject of the illustrations on pages 17–18. [BB92/14605/PW]

Opposite top: Another engraving of Botallack Mine in which the dramatic cliff scenery and the precarious locations of the mine buildings have been exaggerated to a remarkable degree when compared with the photograph on page 17. The foreground with waterwheel, chimney, cart and baskets appears to have been introduced from elsewhere, presumably to accentuate further the drama of the main subject. It is doubtful if any cart could have reached the water's edge in one piece around this locality. [BB71/3764]

Opposite below: A further engraving of Botallack Mine appeared in *The Illustrated London News*, 6 January 1872, together with a paragraph about the mine working in such picturesque scenery. Once again the topography has been made a little more dramatic, but the representation of the mining elements is much more faithful to their actual layout.

An early photograph of The Crowns by C R Lobb in the 'Red Box' collection at the National Monuments Record Centre in Swindon. It probably dates from the 1860s and shows, in the centre, the engine house that contained Pearce's Whim that wound from the Boscawen Diagonal Shaft. The flue from the boiler can be seen running up the hill to a short chimney. To the left is the much older pumping engine house with smoke issuing from its stack. It makes an interesting comparison to the photograph on page 17 that was taken almost 140 years later. [© B E C Howarth-Loomes, BB85/2157B]

A view of Black Tor Falls on the River Meavy, near Princetown, Devon. In the foreground is some massive granite stonework of a medieval blowing house where tin was smelted. A waterwheel on the far side of the house, driven by a short leat from the top of the waterfall, once powered the bellows of the furnace. On the other side of the river, a little further from the water, can be seen the remnants of a second blowing house. Further examples of blowing houses feature in the illustrations on pages 100 and 104.
[AA99/04965/PW]

The site of Whiteworks Mine, near Princetown, Devon, from the west-north-west, looking down the straight causeway of the former tramway towards the site of Lower Stamps. At the near end of the tramway is a depression that marks the collapsed portal of the mine 'adit' from which the ore was drawn. The foreground has been disturbed by centuries of mining, and the leat bringing water to the mine runs a sinuous course this side of the nearest stone wall. To the left of the causeway, and at an angle to it, is a branch of this leat that once fed a pumping waterwheel.
[AA99/04966/PW]

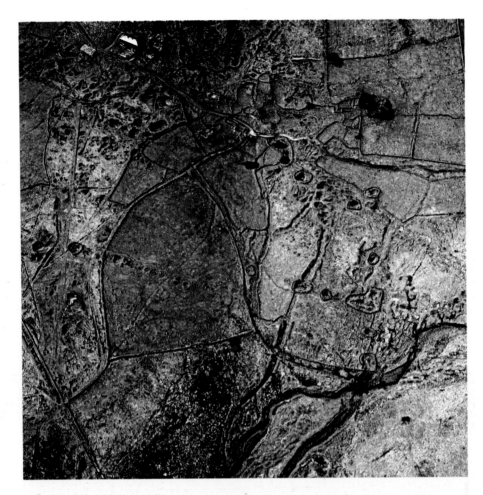

The photographs *above* and *opposite* have been taken with film that is sensitive only to infra-red radiation. The resultant effects are 'false colour' images and the depth and shade of colour is largely related to the degree and type of vegetation cover. Such photographs often enhance the contrasts in both natural and artificial features.

An aerial view of Whiteworks Mine, near Princetown, Devon, from the south-east. The illustration on page 21 was taken from a point immediately above the light bluish rectangle close to the top left corner, looking straight down the line of the tramway that runs almost vertically down this picture. For centuries the area had been streamed for tin, and some of these workings are in the centre at the top of this picture. By the late 18th century the mine was being developed underground, and various test-pits and walled shafts can be seen clearly following lodes. At the top left is the road with a range of mine cottages. This, and many other such images were taken as part of an archaeological survey of Dartmoor. [NMR SX6170/2/456]

Legis Tin Workings, Brisworthy, Devon; an aerial photograph from the south-east. The Legis Lake stream flows down from the top right corner of the picture towards the River Plym that is seen in the lower part of the view. The bottoms of both valleys show clear evidence of generations of tin streaming. The prominent curved line running from the bottom right corner of the photograph is a 19th century leat contouring the hillside. This leat formerly continued for another three miles (5 km) to take water to the tin mine of Yeoland Consols. Roughly parallel with, and to the left of, this leat is a lower and much earlier leat. Both leats cut across a prehistoric enclosed settlement. The round-ended, elongated structures are pillow mounds to accommodate rabbit warrens. [NMR SX5765/6/477]

Opposite page: The view from a mile (1.6 km) west of Zennor, on the north coast of Cornwall, looking westwards across Porthglaze Cove with Gurnard's Head in the background. The large waterwheel pit in the foreground is the lower one of a pair that supplied the power for Carnelloe Mine. The water was brought a considerable distance onto the headland by a leat. [AA98/08998/JOD]

The upper waterwheel of Carnelloe Mine drove the stamps and dressing floors but the dramatic wheelpit is now deteriorating rapidly. The count house nearby is seen in the illustration on page 143. The mine has been out of use since about 1876. [AA98/09000/JOD]

Looking up Trevellas Coombe, St. Agnes. A landscape that has been
modified for centuries in the search for, and extraction of, tin ore. In the
valley bottom every square metre has been disturbed. [AA98/10283/PW]

Opposite top: An apparently rural scene north-east of St. Day showing the close association between farming
and mining. The rushes in the bottom of the valley are indicative of some surface water, but the natural
drainage has been modified dramatically by the digging of the County Adit, taking much of the water underground. In the foreground is the track of the 4-ft gauge Redruth and Chasewater Railway that conveyed the
minerals from the St. Day area to the dock at Devoran in the estuary of the Carnon Valley. On the other side
of the track can be seen one of the structures that have been appearing in recent years to make the open shafts
a little safer for the unwary. [AA98/10278/PW]

Opposite below: Looking eastwards up the hillside in the Tywarnhayle valley, near Porthtowan, towards John's
Engine House. This house was built in 1861 for a 70-inch beam engine that only worked here until 1864. The
engine had come second-hand from Great Hewas Mine, St. Austell, and it went from here to the mine of
Wheal Uny at Redruth. [AA98/08962/PW]

A watercolour created by Beryl Cook in about 1949 as one of the images for volume 4 of the 'Recording Britain' series. It shows a 'Disused tin mine in St. Agnes' and may represent an engine house that was on old workings, previously known as Wheal Friendly, although by that time it was part of West Wheal Kitty, a mine that produced tin and copper, and closed in about 1915. [V&A Picture Library: CT 19003]

Opposite top: The ruins of the compressor house of South Tincroft Mine near Carn Brea. This was built in 1891 to house a steam-powered air compressor by Harvey and Co of Hayle. The compressed air was piped underground to power machinery and to aid ventilation in the mine. [AA98/08965/PW]

Opposite below: It is easy to forget that the stone engine houses that remain today were only a part of the complex of surface buildings that typified a Cornish mine. This commercial postcard of East Pool Mine, between Camborne and Redruth, was post-marked in 1908. East Pool was one of the most profitable and productive of all the Cornish tin mines. To the right of the picture is shown Engine Shaft, which was the principal shaft of the mine until a serious underground collapse occurred in 1921. This scene demonstrates well how many of such buildings were constructed in timber, so that few elements of a complex like this would be expected to survive. [P W collection]

Waste dumps at Wheal Jane, Baldhu, near Truro. In the background is the mill, or treatment plant, with the bank of the
tailings pond to the right. As the waste rock in these heaps
already contains undesirable elements the excavation is allowed
to be used as a dump for modern contaminated waste before it
becomes backfilled and landscaped. Further photographs of
Wheal Jane are included in Chapters 2, 5 and 9. [AA98/10486/PW].

An engine house of South Wheal Frances, south of Camborne. It once contained a 30- or 36-inch beam winding engine that hauled ore from the nearby Pascoe's Shaft, and is unusual in still retaining the walls of its adjoining boiler house. The shaft was sunk in about 1887 to develop part of the Great Flat Lode, one of the greatest tin lodes in Cornwall. In the background can be seen the remains of three other engine houses, all part of Wheal Grenville, for working other parts of the same lode. This engine house became part of the Basset Mines group and is seen again in the picture below. [AA98/10336/PW]

The derelict mine buildings of South Wheal Frances represent two phases of development of the Great Flat Lode south of Camborne. In the distance are the two engine houses of Pascoe's Shaft, the winding engine to the left and the 80-inch pumping engine to the right. In the foreground are the buildings of Marriott's Shaft, erected in about 1900 as part of the Basset Mines. The nearest building housed the winding engine, a twin-cylinder compound steam engine with a large conical drum, built by Holman Bros of Camborne. Behind it is the pumping engine house that contained a unique inverted vertical compound beam engine with 40- and 80-inch cylinders and, to the right, the shared boiler house that is the subject of the illustration on page 186. The Basset Mines only lasted until 1918. [AA98/10332/JOD]

Above: Levant Mine, perched on the cliff top to the west of Geevor, St. Just in Penwith. To the left is the recently restored whim house, or winding house, containing a 24-inch rotative beam engine built by Harvey and Co of Hayle in 1840. The tiny headframe is over Skip Shaft, which was the shaft in which the hoisting was done. The empty engine house was for pumping, and the fencing marks the position of Engine Shaft, directly below where the beam once projected. This was the mine where the infamous man-engine disaster occurred in 1919, and the scene on that day has been reconstructed in the illustration on pages 152–153. [AA98/10337/PW]

Opposite top: Looking eastwards along the main railway line to the east of Camborne station. To the left of the line is the pumping engine house of Wheal Harriett, part of the great Dolcoath Mine. Water to serve a series of mines in this area had been brought in by a long leat in the 18th century and, when the railway was built, an aqueduct had to be constructed. This is visible in front of the engine house. In the background is the prominent hill of Carn Brea with the Basset Monument on the summit. The wall along the right-hand side of the railway cutting marks the site of a 19th-century ropewalk that served the mining industry. [AA98/10419/PW]

Opposite below: Holman Bros of Camborne were renowned for their engineering products. They had their origin in a boiler works at Pool, two miles east (3.2 km) of Camborne, which Nicholas Holman had founded in 1801. The firm built a number of steam engines for the mining industry, but they specialised in compressed-air equipment, and their air-driven rock drills were to be found in metal mines all over the world. Much of the factory, which used to be a major employer in the area, has now disappeared but, adjacent to the main London to Penzance railway line near Trevu Road in Camborne, the faded painted lettering on some of the surviving buildings can still be seen. [AA98/16742/PW]

Looking out in a north-westerly direction over Tuckingmill, a suburb of Camborne, from the top of the derelict treatment plant at South Crofty. The Red River flows through the centre of Tuckingmill, passes beneath the A30 road embankment that is visible on the right-hand side of the picture, and then curves to the left and runs in front of the smooth range of the Reskajeage Downs in the left-hand distance. The whole of this valley was once filled with tin-streaming works that were salvaging fine-grained tin from material that had been discarded from the tin mines upstream. [AA005790/PW]

A view of the South Crofty complex, near Camborne, from the west showing the mill, or treatment plant, the conveyor-ways and concrete ore bins. The mill had been out of use since 1989, when the ore was diverted to Wheal Jane for processing. (*See also* illustrations on pages 113–116). On the right-hand side is the double headframe of Cook's Shaft with the steel ropes passing to each of the two winding engines. These were in continuous use until 1998.
[AA007891/JOD]

Looking westwards from Station Road, Pool, between Camborne and Redruth. In the foreground is a building that was once a miners' dry where the men changed their clothes and hung up any wet items. It was part of the original South Wheal Crofty and probably dates from the 1850s. Behind it is the Robinson's engine house and headframe that represent the development of the mine about fifty years later. In the distance is the enormous Cook's Shaft headframe that marks the last phase of South Crofty. This is a fascinating illustration of the sequential shifting of the focal point of the mine as its mineral potential was realised.
[AA98/01038/PW]

A view of the South Condurrow Mine buildings that now comprise the surface facilities of King Edward Mine, near Camborne. In 1897 this became the practical training ground for students at the internationally renowned Camborne School of Mines. The engine house on the right once contained a 25-inch rotary beam engine for winding, with its boiler house to the left. To the left again is the calciner, with a square chimney. This was for roasting the ore to drive off the sulphides. In the foreground is some salvaged equipment that is the subject of the illustrations on pages 129 and 130. (For further external views of the buildings see the illustrations on page 140 and for scenes inside the buildings see the illustrations on pages 101–103, 105 and 109–111.) [AA98/10633/PW]

The roofscape at Tolgus Tin Streams near Redruth. The colours of the corrugated iron mirror those of the slimes and slurries that are dealt with in the buildings beneath. The taller building in the right-hand background houses the battery of Cornish stamps that is featured in the illustration on page 98. The whole complex has been protected by being 'listed' ie it is included on the statutory list of buildings of 'special architectural and historic interest' for the area.

(*See also* the illustrations on pages 99, 128 and 185.)
[AA98/03118/PW]

A 70-ft 'thickener' beside the mill at Geevor, St. Just in Penwith. It was used to encourage the precipitation of very fine sediment, thus liberating relatively clear water for re-use in the treatment plant. In the background are the remains of the treatment plant associated with the former Levant Mine. Rescorla's Stack, the subject of the illustration on page 39, is the one furthest to the right. [BB91/25652/PW]

A distant view of Geevor Mine from the waste dumps of the former Levant Tin-streaming Works. These works were extracting the very fine tin that had eluded the treatment plants attached to the main mines of Levant and Geevor. The circular stack shows elements commonly seen in the mines of the South-West, the lower part built in local rubble and the upper portion in red brick, often imported from Bridgwater in Somerset, with a decorated corbelled band at the junction. This chimney is sometimes known as Rescorla's Stack after the family that used to operate the streaming works. Since this picture was taken, much clinical landscaping has taken place in the interests of aesthetics and safety. [BB92/14688/PW]

Opposite page: A view of the 'Wild West' of Cornwall, also beside Geevor Mine. It shows how the mining has been superimposed on traditional rural agriculture. The small fields in the background, bounded by granite rubble walls, are typical of much of the Lands End peninsula. [BB92/14691/PW]

A series of parallel conveyors forming part of the compli-
cated process of concentrating the tin at the treatment
plant below the mine at Geevor. [BB92/14660/PW]

Opposite top: A clutch of conveyors north-east of the mill at Geevor in 1991. These were used to distribute
the discarded crushed, unmineralised granite that was a by-product from the mine but proved popular as an
aggregate. In the distance are two of the stacks of Levant Mine. The left-hand one was for the steam-powered
air compressor and the right-hand one was to carry noxious arsenic fumes from the calciner where the ore
was roasted. [BB92/14692/PW]

Opposite below: A view of the area on the cliff top to the east of Levant, looking north-west. The forest of
concrete pillars is all that remains from the latest mill for Levant Mine, erected in 1922, only eight years
before the closure of the whole operation. The mill was a large building, largely timber-clad, but most of the
machinery it contained was bought second-hand. It had been erected on part of the site of earlier dressing
floors. [BB92/14678/PW]

It is sometimes difficult to imagine many of these features of mining landscapes in the days when the mines were prospering. Occasionally images of the past emerge, such as this 19th-century Cornish mining scene in oils. The location is not known but was probably somewhere in the Camborne–Redruth area. Numerous piles of ore are shown, some of the ore is being weighed and recorded in the foreground. The treatment by the artist is naïve but what he captures is precious. There are the obvious signs that the mine is at work and the atmosphere is one of bustling activity.

[Cornish mining scene by English School (19th century) The Royal Institution of Cornwall, Truro, Cornwall, UK/Bridgeman Art Library]

Opposite page: A distant view of South Crofty from the remains of Brea Tin-streaming Works, in the upper course of the Red River, that ceased in the mid-1960s. In the foreground are two concrete structures, a modern development of the traditional 'buddle', used for separating the fine-grained tin mineral, cassiterite, from the gangue, or waste. On the skyline beyond the village of Brea are, from left to right, the South Crofty treatment plant, the Cook's Shaft headframe and the ruined engine houses of the old Cook's Kitchen mine. [AA98/03091/PW]

Standing on the summit of Carn Brea near Redruth, at about 740 feet (225 m) above sea level, is this striking granite monument. It was erected by public subscription to Lord Dunstanville and Basset in 1836. The Basset family resided at Tehidy, north of Camborne, and was one of the main mineral owners of this intensively-mined district. It seems rather ironic that sufficient public money was forthcoming to erect such an expensive memorial to a very rich man who had benefited directly from dues paid by the tin and copper mines that struggled on at the expense of the underpaid and overworked miners and their families. This view is looking northwards and the hill in the distance is St. Agnes Beacon. The monument forms a fine landmark, as is seen in the illustrations on pages 13, 32 and 154. [AA98/10407/PW]

Shafts

A shaft represented the centre of a mine and yet, once the mine has ceased to operate and the headframe has come down, the shaft becomes insignificant in landscape terms. Its location may be marked by an engine house, a heap of waste rock, an open hole or merely a fenced-off area. From time to time the appearance of a fresh hole in the ground is a reminder of the presence of old mine workings for which no record survives, and of the ever-present danger that is posed by abandoned shafts. Many such collapses occur of shafts that have been capped, or even infilled, in the past.

A record has been made of the surviving mine headframes in Cornwall – potent and stark structures that proclaim the link between the everyday world above the surface and the hidden one that lies beneath the ground. Headframes are a threatened species and at least two have disappeared since these photographs were taken.

The headframe over No. 2 Shaft at Wheal Jane. This shaft is 1204 feet (367 m) deep and was used to transport men and materials. When this photograph was taken the mine had already closed, as seen by the absence of hoisting ropes. Subsequently the headframe has been demolished; only the sheave wheels have survived on-site.
[BB95/08655/PW]

A graphic illustration of the dangers of abandoned mine shafts. This particular example is one of the two main shafts at Wheal Jane and it has been well-secured. There are many others, however, that are either open or have been capped poorly in the past. [AA98/10488/PW]

Bickford's Shaft, part of the former South Wheal Crofty, at Pool, near Redruth. A clear example of the potential danger associated with problems of mining in a residential area. In the subsiding wreckage can be seen some of the concrete foundation blocks of the former wooden headframe that used to stand over the shaft, together with steel winding rope. [AA98/10380/PW]

The Robinson's engine house at South
Crofty is much as it was constructed in
1903, apart from the truncation of the
chimney that was carried out soon after
the engine stopped work in 1955. Also
missing is the pump rod that used to
hang the depth of the shaft from the nose
of the engine beam. The headframe has
been replaced in steel and a functional,
unaesthetic modern shed has been added
in front. Images of the beam engine
inside this engine house are shown on
pages 59 and 60. [BB95/09768/JOD]

This modern headframe was designed and erected by
South Crofty staff at Roskear Shaft, Camborne, in 1994–6.
This shaft became important for the working mine in
recent years for upcast ventilation, and also for emergency
egress. One of the two electric winders associated with this
headframe is seen in the illustration on page 68. The
concrete block-work housing the ventilation fan is visible
behind the lower part of the headframe and, in the
distance above it, is the shell of the original 1922 winding
house for the shaft. [AA98/08949/PW]

Modern small-scale buildings that mark Vivian's Shaft of Great Condurrow Mine, Camborne. This is an old shaft with associated shallow workings that have been completely refurbished to provide some of the necessary underground facilities for students of the Camborne School of Mines. To the left of the headframe is the winding house, although the steel hoisting rope has been removed. The central building contains an extractor fan for underground ventilation and the concrete flue can be seen leading to it from the shaft. The illustrations on pages 78 and 83 are of scenes in this mine. [AA98/10635/PW]

Opposite page: The winding engine house at Taylor's Shaft, East Pool Mine, between Camborne and Redruth. This was built in about 1921. Although it is now a shell the two openings through which the winding ropes passed are still visible, with the stain of the thrown-off oil, and even the sliding restraining pulley in place in the upper opening. The Holman Bros twin horizontal steam winding engine came here from Allen's Shaft at Botallack Mine, and was only scrapped in 1974. [AA98/09006//PW]

A small headframe over a shaft in the valley north-west of Cook's Shaft at South Crofty. It was one of the points of access to the all-important adit system that helped to keep the pumping costs down by collecting percolating water and diverting it to the surface some distance down the valley. The pipework and valve below the headframe suggest that this route was used to conduct fine mill tailings from the treatment plant for discharge into the aptly named Red River. The terraces of miners' cottages in the background are on the south-eastern edge of Tuckingmill. This headframe has now been dismantled and removed. [BB97/03984/PW]

Geevor Tin Mines Ltd was formed in 1911 and Victory shaft, begun in 1919, was the main shaft of the mine. In the foreground is an old building that was probably part of the former workings on this site of North Levant Mine. [BB92/14646/PW]

Mount Wellington Mine near St. Day was short-lived. It commenced production in 1976 but was forced to close two years later. After amalgamation with the nearby Wheal Jane to the east it reopened in 1980, but was finally closed in 1991. This view is of the derelict headframe, as much a memorial to tin mining as the venerated engine houses, proudly overlooking the Carnon Valley. In the foreground are the scars left by the removal of the winding engine and house. [BB95/09861/PW]

The wooden headgear over Wethered's Shaft at Geevor, dating from about 1911, that still remains beside the main approach road to the mine. All the mining headframes used to be constructed of timber, but these structures are now rare, and this one has been given statutory protection by being declared a 'listed' building. [AA98/03090/PW]

Treweek's Shaft of the old Boscaswell Downs
Mine eventually became part of Geevor Mine. It
was improved and refurbished and, until 1990,
formed the main access way to an important
section of the mine. To the right is the winding
house and, to the left, the compressor house with
the air receivers. From these the pipes ran that
conveyed the compressed air down the shaft for
power and ventilation. This photograph was taken
in December 1991 and the headframe was
demolished soon afterwards. [BB92/14614/PW]

Opposite page: The stark headframe on Allen's
Shaft at Botallack Mine, St. Just in Penwith. Along
with the winding house to the left, it was erected
in the early 1980s by the Geevor Mine Company
to investigate the potential of this area but, when
the tin price crashed in 1985, it was abandoned
again. The chimney in the background remains
from the sinking of this shaft in 1908 and was for
a Holman Bros twin horizontal steam engine that
was later re-used at Taylor's Shaft, East Pool Mine,
and was only scrapped in 1974. [BB92/14693/PW]

Cook's Shaft at South Crofty, from the west. From this view the headframe can be seen to have been made up from two separate units, each with its pair of winding cables. To the left is the winding house for raising skips of ore and, to the right, is the one for hoisting men and materials. In the foreground is the conveyor for taking ore to the ore bins. [BB95/09707/PW]

Opposite page: The largest wooden headframe to survive in Cornwall is this one at Wheal Concorde, Blackwater, near St. Agnes. The short-lived underground exploration programme was the result of the promising geological assessments for tin that were carried out in the 1960s and 70s. [AA98/08960/PW]

Page 56/57: Cook's Shaft at South Crofty from the south, again showing the winding cables to the two winding houses. The buildings on the right of the photograph are part of the complex that had previously formed the foundry seen on page 136, where many mine castings were produced. [AA000398/PW]

A few shafts still have engines associated with them, some of which are included in this selection of photographs. There are four Cornish beam engines remaining at the tin mines where they last worked; two were pumping engines and two were winding engines, or whims. Also included here are two examples of Cornish boilers. Horizontal steam winders, and their electrically-powered descendants, have not been forgotten. In the past, huge steam-powered compressors used to supply the compressed air that was piped down the shaft to the underground working-places. That generation of compressor has disappeared, but the modern installation at South Crofty has been included as a contrasting equivalent.

Many of the cast-iron engine beams carried the name of the foundry and the year when they were cast. Rather sad collections of inscribed fragments of scrapped beam engines lie outside the two preserved East Pool engine houses between Camborne and Redruth. These four lie against the wall of Taylor's engine house. The oldest one is by the Perran Foundry, dated 1815, and it came from New Sump Shaft at Dolcoath as shown in the illustration on page 14. [BB98/13674/PW]

A photograph of the historic beam engine at Levant Mine, taken in October 1969 by John Parkinson, and now in the 'Red Box' collection at the National Monuments Record Centre in Swindon. After the mine closed in 1930 this was the first engine to be saved by the Cornish Engines Preservation Society. It is a 24-inch engine, later enlarged to 27-inch, built by Harvey and Co of Hayle in 1840, and is thought to be the oldest steam engine in Cornwall. It is a whim, or winding engine, for hoisting ore out of the mine through Skip Shaft. The engine is now in the care of the National Trust and has been restored to working condition by volunteers. [BB76/03568]

The Robinson's Shaft pumping engine at South Crofty is complete, but not open to the public. It was built by Sandys Vivian and Co of Copperhouse, Hayle in 1854, and this is the fourth engine house in which it has been installed. This view is in the middle chamber of the house and shows the top of the cylinder with the piston rod projecting from it. The engine stopped work in 1955 and all the bright-work on it has been heavily greased in order to prevent corrosion. [BB95/09769/JOD]

A boiler lying to the east of Robinson's Shaft at South Crofty. The single large flue that distinguishes the Cornish type of boiler is clearly visible. Such a boiler features on one of the plaques on Richard Trevithick's statue in Camborne (*see* the illustration on page 161). [AA98/10376/PW]

Opposite top: The casing around the base of the 80-inch cylinder in the bottom chamber of the 1854 Robinson's beam engine at South Crofty. The richly decorated cast-iron work reflects the 'gothick' design that was still popular at the time. [BB95/09753/JOD]

Opposite below: Taylor's engine house of East Pool Mine has been preserved and is open to the public. It is the largest of the beam engines in Cornwall and the beam weighs $52\frac{1}{2}$ tons. The bottom chamber of the house is seen here with the valve control gear in the centre, and the wood and brass lagging of the 90-inch cylinder to the right. In the background is the engine man's settle. To the left is the wide, arched cylinder opening, through which the heavy engine parts were hauled into the engine house. The engine was built by Harvey and Co of Hayle, in 1892 and worked at Carn Brea Mines. It was re-erected here in 1924. [BB98/13675/PW]

Opposite page: A Cornish boiler at Michell's Whim, East Pool Mine. The engine house is open to the public. The rotary beam engine inside dates from 1887 and came here new, but this 1926 boiler, by Ruston and Hornsby of Lincoln, was acquired from a laundry in Truro. The boiler is no longer fired, and the engine is now turned by an electric motor. [BB98/13653/PW]

Above: The bottom chamber of Michell's Whim. This view is reminiscent of a chapel with the arched window and the wooden balustraded stairway up to the gallery. The vertical cylinder, 30 inches in diameter, was lagged in order to conserve the heat and then has been painted as Flemish bond brickwork. The engine was built by Holman Bros of Camborne in 1887 and came here new. Out of use since 1921 the house and engine is now open to the public. [BB98/13652/PW]

Left: In the capstan house at Robinson's Shaft of South Crofty this steam crab winch still remains. It is a very important survival and yet it receives scant attention. Built by Harvey and Co of Hayle in 1882, it must have come here second-hand. The engine was used for raising and lowering maintenance materials in the shaft. [AA95/02870/JOD]

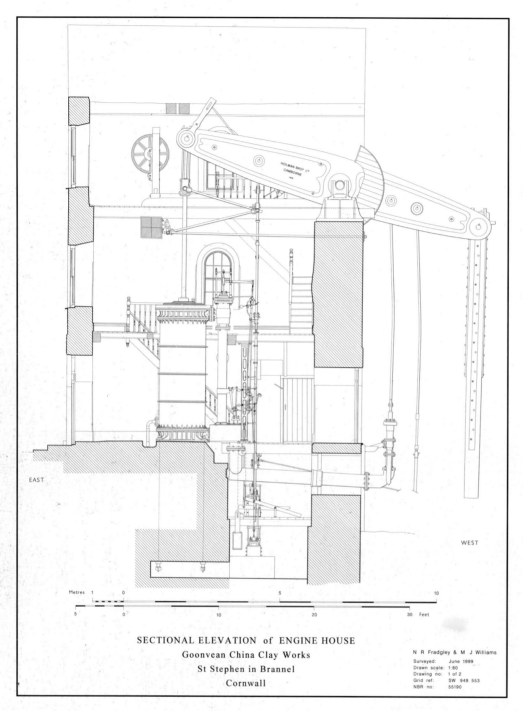

SECTIONAL ELEVATION of ENGINE HOUSE
Goonvean China Clay Works
St Stephen in Brannel
Cornwall

N R Fradgley & M J Williams
Surveyed: June 1999
Drawn scale: 1:80
Drawing no: 1 of 2
Grid ref: SW 949 553
NBR no: 55190

It requires a scale drawing to appreciate the intricacies of a Cornish beam engine and to understand the integration of the various elements. This is a record that has been produced by English Heritage of the engine and house at Goonvean prior to their removal. The main beam was a replacement following a breakage. At the time of publication the fate of this engine is uncertain.

Opposite page: The bottom chamber of the Goonvean engine house makes a dramatic comparison with the engines in Cornwall that have been preserved. Abandoned and neglected, the only attention that it has received has been the stripping of the asbestos lagging to expose the massive cast-iron work of the 50-inch cylinder – a rare sight. The engine was erected in this new house, its fourth home, in 1910. Built by Harvey and Co of Hayle in 1863 it worked successively at three tin mines in St. Agnes (Penhalls, Trevaunance and Gooninnis Mines), before coming to this china-clay pit. [BB98/21547/PW]

The remains of the twin-horizontal steam winder at Roskear Shaft, east of Camborne. This shaft, also known as New Dolcoath, was started in 1922 by the Dolcoath Mine Company, two years after that famous mine had closed. After many years of dereliction it was eventually re-equipped by South Crofty men. The engine was originally a single-drum winder, built by Worsley Mesnes of Wigan in 1897, but a second drum was manufactured locally and added to it. Most of the engine was scrapped many years ago. (The house in which this relic survives is shown in the background of the illustration on page 47). [BB95/08617/JOD]

Opposite page: The south winder at Cook's Shaft, South Crofty, showing the pair of drums and the powerful brake linkage. This is the hoist that operated the man-riding cages. It was constructed by Fullarton in 1959 and came here in 1970 from New Monkton Collieries. [AA000421/PW]

The winder driver at the controls in his cabin at the refurbished Roskear Shaft. The winder is an electric, hydraulic single-drum machine by M B Wild of about 1980–2. It used to be the spillage hoist for Clemow's Shaft at Wheal Jane. Roskear Shaft was totally re-equipped by South Crofty men in 1994–6 as an emergency shaft for the mine. [AA98/08953/PW]

Inside the large, double-range, timber-framed corrugated iron shed at South Crofty. It was originally associated with the adjoining foundry and the exterior is shown in the illustration on page 137. Among items stored here is a portable electric winch that has seen service in the construction of a mine decline. [AA000425/PW]

The modern air compressors at Cook's Shaft of South Crofty are much smaller than their predecessors. The Ingersoll Rand 'Centac' is a centrifugal compressor of 5,500 cubic feet (156 cu m) per minute capacity and it is supported by three smaller machines. The air is piped down the shaft to drive much of the underground machinery and, at times, to aid ventilation. [AA000417/PW]

Underground

An attempt has been made to capture the main stages in the mining of the tin ore, with images of some of the men who were about to have to come to terms with a complete change in lifestyle with the closure of the last tin mine.

SOUTH CROFTY MINES RESCUE

Three members of the mines rescue team beside Cook's Shaft at South Crofty. This is a dedicated team of volunteers, each of whom has to have a first-aid certificate, at least two years of underground experience, and be prepared for selfless training and commitment. They are wearing their Proto mark IV breathing apparatus and rescue equipment. [AA000401/PW]

Opposite page: After hours spent drilling holes above his head in a 'stope', or working-place on a lode, a South Crofty miner takes a rest before loading the holes with explosive. [AA95/02850/PW]

Above: An adit in the cliff to the west of Perranporth. This is a horizontal tunnel that comes out to the surface. It may have been cut to explore a specific mineral vein, or lode, or it could have been to drain the workings. Often an adit fulfilled both functions. By having the portal close to high tide level the maximum depth of natural drainage in a mine working could be achieved. [AA005892/PW]

Left: Inside the same adit, looking towards the portal. The boulders and rubbish on the floor are indicative of the ferocity of some of the storms on this coast. The rock consists of ancient sediments that have been altered by the heat and pressure from the granite below. It shows a certain amount of fracturing although no mineralisation can be seen. Adits are extremely dangerous and sometimes connect with flooded workings below. [AA005894/PW]

A view along an adit in Rosevale Mine near Zennor. In its scale this view is more typical of a traditional Cornish tin mine than any other picture in this book. In general no more waste rock was removed than was necessary for ease of working. The adit is following a lode, as is shown by the irregular roof, the sheared nature of the right-hand wall, the curvature of the tunnel and, in the background, the chute for loading broken ore into wagons. Beyond the wagon is a mucking machine, used for loading a wagon with rock lying on the floor ahead. Rosevale is a reopened former tin mine kept in impeccable condition, but it is unlikely to have had anything as sophisticated as a mucking machine in any of its previous working phases. Clean granite can be seen in the left-hand foreground. [AA95/02591/JOD]

Opposite page: Another view in Rosevale Mine near Zennor. Here the lode was productive and has been worked, or stoped, above the adit but the ground has been left where it was uneconomic. At the far end of the stope the steeply-dipping, dark-coloured lode has split and the adit curves to follow the right-hand branch. Wooden 'stulls' have been left in place to give some support to the hanging wall. [AA95/02603/JOD]

Above: Occasionally the lodes were very branched and complex, or the mineralisation was disseminated over a wide area. If the grade was high enough it was sometimes economic to remove the intervening barren or low-grade material with the ore, taking advantage of bulk-mining techniques. Such stopes, or places from which the ore has been removed, could be vast. Here is one that became accessible when South Crofty drained the flooded workings of the neighbouring East Pool Mine. The scale of this artificial cavern is indicated by the human figure in the brightly-illuminated area to the left-hand side. [AA95/02879/JOD]

Right: As mines became deeper, and with advances in technology, the pumping machinery was often under pressure for modernisation or replacement. Relics of old pump-work are rare, but here some remain, deep in Robinson's Shaft at South Crofty. Long out of use, it was once powered by the now-preserved beam engine, however its removal for scrap is uneconomic, despite its enormous size and weight. This picture conveys something of the difficult conditions that prevailed in these mine shafts. [AA95/02886/PW]

Looking along the main lode in Great Condurrow Mine, Camborne. This eventually became the underground part of King Edward Mine, a valuable training ground for students at the world-famous Camborne School of Mines. Here the lode is almost vertical and wide, and has been productive in the past. In addition to tin the mineralisation comprised sulphides of iron and copper, and the oxidation of these has produced rusty deposits on the walls. The pipes fixed to the right-hand wall carry water and compressed air to the working-places and the ducting on the left is to aid ventilation. [AA98/10614//PW]

The sheer granite of the quarry at Bodrivial near Camborne was a perfect proving ground for the rock drilling equipment that was developed and sold all over the world by Holman Bros of Camborne and it became a test mine for their products. From the floor of the quarry an extensive underground system was developed in the massive granite, purely for equipment testing purposes. The mine has become a training ground for Camborne School of Mines students. The quarry faces are now being reclaimed by liverworts, pennywort and foxgloves. [AA98/08940/PW]

An abandoned ventilation fan that had been submerged by water almost a third of a mile (520 m) deep for about seventy years after the closure of East Pool Mine. Mud-covered relics like this suddenly became visible when the mine in which they were used was drained to become an extension of South Crofty but, since the drainage pumps have been switched off, they have disappeared beneath the water once again. [AA95/02874/PW]

A painting by Terence Cuneo of the Holman test mine at Bodrivial, near Camborne, in December 1949. It features in *Cornish Engineers*, a book published by Holman Bros Ltd in 1951, and the original is said to have hung in the Holman boardroom at Camborne. As a rare example of a painting of an underground tin-mining scene, the meticulous attention to detail suggests that it may have been painted from photographs to a large degree.

A miner about to begin his shift at Cook's Shaft. He has his personal tally in his hand, ready to pass it over before he goes underground. He will collect it again on his return to the surface at the end of his shift. Two aspects of his clothing differ from that of most coal miners; it is his own, and it is clearly for working in hot conditions. [AA000461/JOD]

A man waiting for the cage to take him underground at Cook's Shaft early on a bright winter morning. This and the remaining photographs in this chapter were taken at South Crofty Mine, near Camborne.
[AA95/02824/JOD]

An unusual painting of an underground scene in mixed media by Graham Sutherland (1903–80). He was an official war artist who came from the coal-mining district of Castleford in West Yorkshire, and was interested in portraying the extractive industries. This semi-abstract work entitled 'Tin Mine: A Declivity' dates from 1942. It shows what appears to be a distant miner at the end of a well-lit tunnel with very rounded walls. The miner is attached to a long rope that passes through an eye-bolt above a small mine wagon. What he has captured vividly is the orange colouration that was so typical of these mines when they were at work.
[Tin Mine: A Declivity, 1942 (mixed media on paper) by Graham Sutherland (1903–80) Leeds Museums and Galleries (City Art Gallery) UK/Bridgeman Art Library]

An underground room in King Edward Mine (formerly Great Condurrow Mine) near Camborne – as clean an environment as can be found underground. This is a reminder of the necessity of adequate first-aid facilities and procedures in mining. It has always been a dangerous way of life, and accidents were all too frequent. [AA98/10615/PW]

Opposite page: The tally board showed which miners were underground and the chalked numbers indicated the area in which each was working (measured in fathoms of depth). Most, but not all, of the miners have traditional Cornish names. [AA95/02814/JOD]

With the involvement of international mining interests, and the increase in national safety regulations, eventually it became necessary for every person going underground to have a respirator with him at all times. This was to facilitate breathing in case there should be an inrush of gas into the mine. On returning to surface the respirator, invariably unused, was wiped clean and returned to the rack. [BB95/09732/PW]

A miner removing his lamp from
the charging rack before going on
shift underground. [AA000466/PW]

Opposite page: Miners preparing to leave the dawn sunlight and enter the cage at Cook's Shaft. [AA95/02827/JOD]

Above: The lander at the top of Cook's Shaft was also responsible for the charging of lamp batteries, and he is seen here plugging the lamps that have just come off shift into the charging racks. The skullcap was the traditional form of headgear that was generally worn beneath a hard hat and an 18th-century example is seen in the illustration on page 165.
[BB95/09711/PW]

Right: The double-deck man-riding cage is about to take the men underground at Cook's Shaft. The men on the lower deck are handing their brass tallies to the lander, who will ensure that they are hung on the tally board.
[AA95/02816/PW]

One of the underground stations of Cook's Shaft. The lower deck of the double-deck cage is in use. Each deck can carry either men or a small underground wagon. The safety gate on the cage has been lifted off and the one at the station has been opened. Before the cage can be moved both gates must be in position and the correct signal must have been sent to the winder driver, using the button mounted on the unit that is visible between the helmets of the two men, and the same signal rung back in acknowledgement. This cage is counterbalanced with another in the shaft compartment immediately to the left. The two more compartments, to the left again, are for the counterbalanced skips in which the ore is hoisted. A vertical timber can be seen to project into both sides of each of the four shaft compartments. These timbers act as guides to prevent lateral movement, and the cages and skips have a rebate on each side to accommodate the guides. The cage is the vital link between two very different worlds. [AA95/02856/JOD]

The Robinson's Shaft station at the 290 fathom (530 m) level with the three-compartment shaft in the background. The left-hand section carries the services – water, electricity and compressed air. The cage is to the right and its counterbalance is in the middle. The condition of the track shows that this level is out of production. [AA95/02885/JOD]

Below; Left: The board indicating the signals to be sent to the winder driver by the cage tender in Robinson's Shaft. On receipt of a signal the winder driver would repeat it in acknowledgement, giving the cage-tender time to ring again if there was any misunderstanding or problem, before the cage was hoisted to the required level. Such a board was displayed at every shaft station. [BB95/09747/PW]

Right: The code of signals board for Cook's Shaft. This shaft used to be called 'New Cook's Kitchen Shaft' to distinguish it from the old Cook's Kitchen Mine, with its ruined engine houses, a short distance to the south. The board is signed by Mr N K Kitto who was the manager of South Crofty from 1958 to 1963. He had been seriously injured in an accident in Robinson's Shaft in 1940. [BB98/13654/PW]

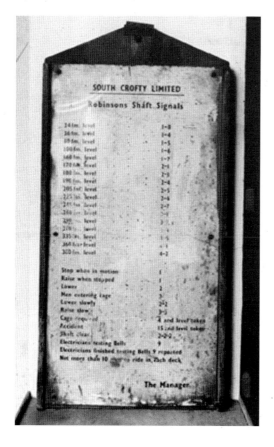

CODE OF SIGNALS	NEW COOK'S KITCHEN SHAFT
1-6	80 FATHOM LEVEL
1-7	148 " "
2-1	175 " "
2-3	195 " "
2-5	205 " "
2-6	225 " "
2-7	245 " "
3-2	290 " "
3-4	315 " "
3-5	340 " "
4-1	360 " "
4-2	380 " "
4-3	380 SLUDGING X CUT
4-4	380 LOADING STATION
1-3	RAISE TO NEXT LEVEL
1-2	LOWER TO NEXT LEVEL
1	STOP (WHEN HOIST IN MOTION)
1	RAISE (WHEN HOIST STOPPED)
2	LOWER
3	MEN ENTERING CAGE
2-2	LOWER SLOWLY
3-3	RAISE SLOWLY
4 & LEVEL SIGNAL	CAGE REQUIRED
15 & LEVEL SIGNAL	ACCIDENT

SIGNED
N.K.KITTO
MANAGER

A miner operating a compressed-air drill in a stope. The dark, altered rock contains disseminated tin mineralisation and it is to be removed by drilling and blasting. The drill is stabilised by the 'air-leg' in the foreground, and water and compressed air are fed to the machine through the hoses to the left. The water flushes the cuttings out of the drill hole and the release of the compressed air causes the small area of mist just above the drill. The noise in such a confined space is intense. [AA98/10572/JOD]

Holes have been drilled into the ore above and the miner is blowing explosive into these with compressed air. This is a shrinkage stope in which the miners are standing on broken ore that has been blasted down on the previous shift. Approximately 15 per cent of mine ore at South Crofty came from stopes, or working-places on the lode, of this type. The structure of the steeply-dipping lode can be seen clearly where the rock has been hosed down. Most of the tin is disseminated in the dark material that forms the right-hand part. Most of the left-hand portion is barren quartz that is a later addition to the lode. [AA95/02847/PW]

A closer view of miners blowing explosives into the holes with compressed air. The electric wires hang from detonators inside the holes and these are eventually connected up and then fired by remote control. This photograph shows the wet and muddy conditions in which some of the miners have to work. [AA95/02846/JOD]

In some places in South Crofty the distribution of mineralised ground produces a complex zone from which it is economical to extract the ore by a bulk mining method. Fans of holes are drilled to predetermined patterns deep into the rock of a large ore-body. The holes are then packed with explosives and detonated sequentially by remote control. The accuracy of the direction, inclination and depth of each drill hole is vital to the efficiency of the operation. Long-hole stopes produced about 75 per cent of the ore from the mine. Here the driller is making the final adjustment to his long-hole drill. [AA95/02839/JOD]

A mucking machine in operation in a drive at South Crofty. It is of a larger variety than the one seen in the illustration on page 74–75 and is operating here in a development heading big enough to be used for mechanised mining. Powered by compressed air fed through the hose, the machine acts as a digger and, when the bucket at the front is full, its load of rock is thrown over the top into a wagon immediately behind it. The deep red colour shows that this drive is following a lode. If the rock contains sufficient tin it will be treated as ore and be hoisted to the surface so that the metal can be extracted. If the tin content is too low it will be discarded as waste. Such headings are extended by a sequence of drilling, blasting, mucking and extending the track, and they contributed up to 10 per cent of the ore from the mine. [AA95/02831/JOD]

After the ore has been blasted down it descends to a chute or draw-point on the level below. This draw-point below a long-hole stope is large enough for a rubber-tyred front-end loader to be used. Power is obtained from the trailing compressed-air hose. The operator is about to attack the pile of ore where the photographer is standing. Once the bucket is full the loader is reversed and the load of ore is thrown over the top of the machine into one of the wagons in the background. The driver of the electric locomotive ensures that the wagon is conveniently positioned for loading. [AA98/10570/PW]

Above: The battery-powered locomotive pulls the wagons of ore from the loading point to the ore-pass near the main shaft. Here the driver is drawing into position ready for a loaded wagon to be tipped. [AA98/10568/JOD]

Left: The ore-pass on one of the levels where the loaded wagons are halted. One by one, the loads of ore are tipped into the chute. This large mine wagon on the right has been caught in the act of being side-tipped, throwing the ore down onto the 'grizzley' – a grid to prevent any oversize blocks entering the ore-pass. The ore drops down to a crusher that reduces the size of the material further before it is hoisted to the surface by skip. [AA007997/JOD]

Sometimes it is necessary to hoist waste rock to the surface and wagons full of rock are tipped into a second chute. This is a close-up of the steel doors controlling the descent of broken rock into the chute. The doors are retracted by hydraulic pistons, thus releasing the rock and allowing it to drop down into the crusher, before it is hoisted up the shaft in a skip. [AA98/10577/JOD]

A pair of miners at South Crofty about to enter their workplace. Smoking generally poses no threat in tin mines. [AA98/10578/JOD]

Looking up the long underground conveyor that carries the tin ore up the 25 per cent gradient decline from the 470 fathom (860 m) to the 400 fathom (732 m) level – the lowest level from which it can be hoisted in the shaft. Beyond the picture to the right are the tracks and walkway of the decline. [AA007998/JOD]

A group of miners having a lunch break in a station beside the decline, deep underground. The walls are of good clean granite. Beyond the screen on the right-hand side sits the operator of the electric hoist for moving materials up and down the track on the decline. [AA98/10576/JOD]

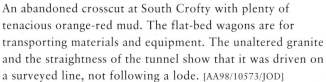

An abandoned crosscut at South Crofty with plenty of tenacious orange-red mud. The flat-bed wagons are for transporting materials and equipment. The unaltered granite and the straightness of the tunnel show that it was driven on a surveyed line, not following a lode. [AA98/10573/JOD]

A disused drive following one of the lodes on the 260 fathoms (475 m) level in the Robinson's section of South Crofty. Some of the rock is dangerously loose and is therefore supported. The larger pipe on the left-hand side carries compressed air and the smaller one contains water. [AA95/02882/PW]

Another abandoned drive at South Crofty following a tin-bearing lode. This is shown by its irregular course, the sheared nature of the wall rock and the presence of the timber chutes. The chutes were for filling wagons with ore from the stope above, indicating that the lode here was productive. After exhaustion of the ore the chutes were blocked off and the track was removed. [AA95/02881/PW]

Processing the Ore

The tin-bearing mineral, cassiterite, generally has a greasy, greyish-brown appearance in a specimen of ore when it is of high grade and of a fairly coarse grain size. In general, however, it is virtually invisible, being fine-grained and masked by various dark minerals in the rock. A mystique has therefore developed around the traditional task of extracting tin from rocks and gravels, and more particularly in tin dressing, the art of the final stages of concentration of the tin ore.

Tin ore from the mine needs to be crushed and ground just fine enough to liberate the particles of cassiterite. These particles are then concentrated by various methods, most of which rely on the higher density of the tin-bearing mineral compared with the barren material. The challenge has always been the economic extraction from the ore of the maximum percentage of tin that is present. Any tin that is too fine-grained will be lost in the residues, or tailings. In the past the tailings from the mines were merely discharged. The resulting sediments in the watercourses downstream from the mines became the raw material for the tin-streaming operations that specialised in salvaging tin of the very finest grain size.

Even though the commercial exploitation of tin has now ceased, a wide range of relics can still be found. These range from the medieval blowing houses of Dartmoor to the modern treatment plants associated with the most recent deep mines. Preserved historic machinery, equipment and techniques can be seen and appreciated at a few sites and occasionally, one or two may be demonstrated. At other locations relics lie forgotten, sometimes being reclaimed by nature. The images presented by tin-ore processing therefore show a surprising variety.

Opposite page: The tin-streaming works at Tolgus, near Redruth, has an impressive battery of Cornish stamps. This battery is in workable condition and has a geared drive from a high-breast waterwheel. The ore is fed down a chute on the far side of the stamps and the fine material is washed out from the cast-iron boxes in the foreground. The cams are staggered in the barrel to even out the action. [BB98/13519/JOD]

Above: A rock that has been used as an ancient anvil for the water-powered hammers that broke down the tin ore. Such arrangements were the precursors of the Cornish stamps and the stones are recognised by the cup-shaped depressions in them, frequently in threes as seen here. In Cornwall these relics have often been referred to as Jews' praying stones. This example is at the tin-streaming works at Tolgus, Redruth. [AA98/03117/PW]

Left: A rare example of a tin mining scene that has been chosen as the subject for a work of art. It shows a battery of Cornish stamps, worked by a waterwheel. Such stamps were constructed in large numbers in south-west England, mainly for treating tin ore, and they became well-known in metal-mining areas in various parts of the world. Very few have survived. The way in which they operated is seen more clearly in some of the later photographs. The action of the stamps crushed the ore and made the separation of the tin-bearing material possible. Subsequent concentration processes would have taken place on the dressing floors that once occupied the foreground of this scene. This battery of stamps was probably somewhere in West Cornwall and was clearly derelict at the time. There appears to have been some later extraction of ground in the lower part of the picture, presumably in a reworking phase to reclaim some of the tin that had been lost here through the years. The picture is a late 19th-century gouache by Oswald Sickert (1828–85) entitled 'A Cornish Tin Mine'. [V&A Picture Library: CT 61620]

The ruins of a medieval blowing house, where the concentrated tin ore was smelted, at Week Ford, near Holne, on Dartmoor. A waterwheel once occupied the pit in which the tree to the left is now growing. This wheel operated bellows for a small furnace that would have yielded tin metal. The massive block of granite in the right-hand foreground is another example of a base for the primitive water-powered stamps that crushed the ore. The three worn depressions can be seen clearly. [AA98/10397/PW]

Because of its unusual shape this tapering granite trough at Bosliven, St. Buryan has the distinction of being classified as a grade II 'listed' building. It is thought to be an ancient 'buddle' for concentrating tin-bearing sands. Similarly shaped buddles are known to have been constructed in medieval times. They made use of a stream of water to remove the lightest, and therefore tin-free, material. Similar examples are shown in use in the illustrations on page 13. It is difficult to see how this particular trough could have been so used because both ends are closed, so that its purpose remains a mystery. [AA99/06869/MHR]

A pair of 'kieves' at the King Edward Mine. These, too, were once standard pieces of tin-dressing equipment for concentrating fine-grained tin. Each kieve contained slurry that was kept agitated by a rotating stirrer. At the same time the side of the kieve would have been thumped with a hammer at regular intervals. The contained sediment gradually sorted itself with the highest concentration of tin at the bottom and the waste at the top. [AA98/10591/PW]

A circular, or rotary, convex 'buddle' that was used for concentrating fine-grained tin ore in the mill at the King Edward Mine, near Camborne, and was typical of practice around 1900. Tin-bearing slurry was introduced in the centre and, as it flowed outwards, the sediment was deposited. The heaviest material, containing the most tin, would tend to be dropped first, with the waste being taken out to the periphery. Brushes, suspended from a frame, rotated constantly, enhancing the separation. Eventually the deposited material would be dug out as different fractions, the richest part being closest to the centre. [AA98/10607/PW]

Opposite page: The invention of the flotation cell revolutionised ore processing worldwide. It was developed to remove the sulphide minerals in the ore and this early example is at the King Edward Mine. Chemicals were added to the ore slurry that gave the sulphide minerals a particular affinity with air and, by the use of a fast-spinning rotary stirrer, the sulphide minerals were floated off as a froth. In the processing of tin ore the presence of sulphide minerals was sometimes a serious problem. (A bank of modern flotation cells is shown in operation in the illustration on page 118.) [AA98/10606/PW]

A remarkable site of a crazing mill and blowing house at Gobbett, near Holne, Dartmoor. Crazing mills used millstones to grind the ore to a powder to release fine-grained cassiterite, so that it could then be concentrated and smelted to produce ingots of tin. It appears that all these operations were carried out here. The pair of granite millstones is visible, one at the top and one at the bottom of the site. Two granite mould stones, into which the liquid tin was poured, can also be seen. One is on the right, just beyond the nearer millstone, and the other is in shadow close to the left-hand edge of the picture. [AA98/10410/PW]

Even finer-grained tin could be concentrated on a round frame such as this rare survival at the King Edward Mine, dating from about 1906. The tin-bearing slurry flowed in a channel around the outside rim and, with the aid of the little adjustable wooden toggles, a steady supply was introduced all around the circular rotating deck. The waste material washes over the surface and into the centre but the heavier minerals tend to be deposited on the deck. In the background can be seen a long brush that sweeps the tin concentrate towards the centre continually as the frame rotates and the enriched material is captured separately below. Scores of such contrivances typified the old tin-streaming works that formerly extracted the finest-grained tin in the valleys around Camborne and Redruth. [AA98/10593/PW]

Another apparatus for reclaiming extremely fine-grained tin from the streams below Camborne and Redruth was the 'rag frame'. Once used in their hundreds, none has survived. Here in the King Edward Mine a small bank of rag frames has been constructed recently to demonstrate the principle. The tin-bearing slurry was passed over the frame and the heaviest fraction would tend to be deposited on it. By a cleverly controlled counterbalance system water would be allowed to fill a container slowly until it tripped a mechanism, tipped the frame, and flushed off any deposited material into a separate channel before reverting to its normal position again. [AA98/10608/PW]

The Cornish stamps at Blue Hills in Trevellas Coombe, St. Agnes has been brought back into use and shows clearly how it operated, as only half has been reinstated. The cast-iron barrel is an extension of the shaft of a waterwheel on the other side of the stone wall. As the barrel rotates in an anticlockwise direction the cams lift projections on the six vertical iron lifters. At the top of its travel the cam automatically disengages, the lifter falls by gravity, and the large iron head at its base pulverises the ore beneath. The waterwheel that drives this stamps is the subject of the illustration on page 128. [AA98/10295/PW]

Unique amongst the relics of Cornish stamps is a small wooden battery at West Ruthern Farm, Withiel. Its latter use was to crush bone although the design, and probably the iron cams and heads, must have come from a tin stamps, of which there were several fairly locally. This view shows the top of the wooden lifters. [AA98/3067/PW]

The lower part of the stamps at West Ruthern Farm. The three iron stamp heads can be seen at the bottom of the wooden lifters and, at the top of the photograph, the iron cams projecting from the wooden stamps barrel. [AA98/03072/PW]

A Cornish stamps, reconstructed on its present site in 1983, stands near the entrance drive to Geevor Mine at St. Just in Penwith. This was formerly Lock Stamps, Ludgvan, and had been derelict for very many years. With the move from its traditional site it has lost some of its integrity and character, although it is certainly much easier to access and its working principles are now clearly visible. Standing unprotected, exposed to the salt-laden winds from the Atlantic, how long will such a monument survive? [AA98/03081/PW]

An old model of a rotative beam engine driving
Cornish stamps in the museum at Geevor Mine.
Somewhat crude and out of scale, the engine only
operates eight heads of stamps instead of perhaps ten
times that number for a full-sized version. Few of the
many beam engine models depict this once very noisy
aspect of tin processing. [BB98/13707/PW]

Opposite page: The Californian stamps was a development from the Cornish stamps. The difference between
the two can be appreciated by comparing the illustration on page 111 with the illustration on page 106. The
only large example to have survived in Cornwall is at the King Edward Mine near Camborne. This picture
shows an ore wagon in the position from where it would have tipped the tin ore onto the 'grizzley' – a screen
to prevent oversize material feeding the stamps below. [AA98/10592/PW]

The main mechanical part of the same Californian stamps. The drive to the belt wheel in the background was originally from a steam engine. The stamps barrel has become merely a shaft carrying enlarged curved cams and, because the five lifters and the heads below are now circular in section, they will be rotated as they are being lifted. This was a more sophisticated version than the Cornish stamps. It was more efficient in operation and the wear of parts was more even. [AA98/10590/PW]

Opposite page: A view of the timber frame-work that surrounds the Californian stamps of King Edward Mine. Erected in about 1906, it is typical of the massive, high quality timberwork that characterised most of these mining operations. [AA98/10600/PW]

The frame of a battery of stamps in the shell of a building perched
on the cliff top below Geevor. The overshot waterwheel that
powered it used to turn in a wheel pit to the left, and the wheel
shaft was extended to form the stamps barrel as it ran the length of
the frame from the rectangular shaft hole. That these were Californian, and not Cornish, stamps is shown by the profile of the rebates
in the upper horizontal bar of the frame. These accommodated
lifters that were circular, instead of rectangular. [AA98/10240/PW]

Opposite page: A derelict 'classifier' in the mill at South Crofty. A classifier is a method of separating larger
and denser particles by dragging them mechanically against a flow of liquid. In this spiral classifier it is
achieved by the steady upward drag from a helical screw in an inclined trough of pulp, or suspended material.
[AA007942/PW]

Page 114: A relatively recent introduction into tin processing have been banks of spirals. These examples are
in the derelict mill at South Crofty. As fine-grained tin-bearing material is washed down the spiral the heavier
tin-rich particles have a different trajectory from that of the lighter sterile fraction so that they can be separated as a concentrate at the bottom. [AA007944/PW]

A general view in the mill at South Crofty. In the background, the conveyor which fed the ore via a hopper into a secondary crusher can be seen. The crushed material then passed through the rotary washer. Heavy media separation was a process, now superseded, in which grains of ferrosilicon, with a fairly high specific gravity, were used in suspension to float off much of the lighter barren waste rock which was to be discarded. In the foreground are the machines which were involved in the recovery of the used ferrosilicon. To the right is a drum magnetic separator that utilised the high magnetic susceptibility of ferrosilicon to salvage it for re-use. To the left is a 'densifier', a device that separated ferrosilicon from rock particles by their difference in specific gravity. [AA007940/PW]

The area beneath the washer in the crusher house at the south end of the derelict treatment plant at South Crofty. It is indicative of the poor condition of this part of the plant. Passing across the scene is one of a series of conveyors that carried the tin-bearing ore. [AA007941/PW]

Inside the derelict mill at South Crofty showing banks of shaking tables. Such tables were the mainstay of tin separation. A detail of a similar table in operation in the mill at Wheal Jane is shown in the illustration, *opposite top*. [AA007943/PW]

A view of some of the last loads of South Crofty ore which have been trucked for ten miles (16 km) from the mine and now await treatment at Wheal Jane. This ore is crushed in the crusher house in the background and then passed up the conveyor to the fine ore dump on the right-hand side. From here an overland conveyor takes the ore to the mill in the distance. [AA98/10482/PW]

An aerial view of the mill at Wheal Jane with the overland conveyor bringing the crushed ore in the background. In the lower part of the picture is the entrance drive with the weighbridge and, below this, the stream conveying the tailings to the tailings pond. The circular structure nearby is a water tank. The similar one to the right of the main building is a 'thickener' that settles out fine sediment and produces additional relatively clear water. (This thickener is seen in the illustration on page 119). In the top right-hand corner of the picture are various sheds, some of which contain samples from the exploration and assessment phases of the former mine, as seen in the illustrations on pages 168 and 169. [NMR 15886-21]

A shaking table in operation in the mill at Wheal Jane. The suspension of fine-grained ore is being introduced in the top right-hand corner and the water flows over the table from the top. The shaking of the table and the natural flow over the slightly rippled surface of the deck cause the minerals to separate. The tin is concentrated in the heaviest light-brown material to the left and is drawn off separately. The dark bands are fairly heavy iron-rich minerals. To the right is the lighter waste fraction. [BB95/08638/PW]

Left: The removal of sulphide minerals from the tin ore at Wheal Jane is achieved by banks of flotation cells. After the addition of special chemicals the pulp is whipped up and the sulphide particles are attracted to air bubbles. This enables them to form a froth that can be taken off. This method has revolutionised many ore-treatment plants throughout the world and has become much more sophisticated since it was pioneered in Cornwall in the early years of the 20th century. (An early flotation cell is seen in the illustration on page 102.) [AA98/10477/MHR]

Below: Ball mills in the mill at Wheal Jane are reducing the size of ore fragments to release more of the tin. They rotate fast, containing a mixture of ore, steel balls and water, and are part of a continuous grinding process. [AA98/10448/MHR]

A 'thickener' beside the mill at Wheal Jane. It is used for precipitating very fine sediment and liberating relatively clear water for re-use, providing about 50 per cent of the water requirements of the plant. Fifty feet (15.24 m) in diameter, it was originally situated beside the treatment plant at South Crofty. Its position relative to the Wheal Jane mill can be seen in the illustration on page 117. [AA98/10510/PW]

The pile of reddish tin ore, fresh from underground at South Crofty, lying against the concrete-ore bins of the old plant. Latterly this ore is loaded into lorries and taken ten miles (16 km) to Wheal Jane to be processed. [AA000409/PW]

The tally, chalked on the wall of the concentrate storage shed at Wheal Jane, records the number of bucketfuls of the front-end loader that have gone into consignments of concentrate leaving the plant. [BB95/08623/PW]

Tailings being discharged into the artificial dam at Wheal Jane. The greenish water has been pumped from the abandoned mine of Wheal Jane and lime has been added in order to precipitate the undesirable elements dissolved in it. [AA98/10481/PW]

Opposite page: Small ingots of tin at Wheal Jane that have been produced from the South Crofty ore. These are remelted, purified and then used to make the local tin jewellery. No large-scale commercial tin smelting has been carried out in Cornwall for more than seventy years. The ingots shown here represent the last stage in the processing of the tin ore and also the final phase in the legacy of Cornish tin production. They contrast strongly with the traditional ingots seen in the illustration on page 174. [BB98/21344/PW]

The grey pile of final tin concentrate in the mill at Wheal Jane. After being sampled this concentrate will be sent to Malaysia or India to be smelted into metallic tin. The powder contains approximately 60 per cent tin. [AA98/10470/MHR]

Taken soon after the final closure of Geevor Mine, St. Just in Penwith, this view shows two Hardinge ball mills inside the coarse sand section of the treatment plant. These mills contain steel balls that are spun round with fairly fine-grained ore fragments and some water in order to release fine-grained cassiterite from the ore as it is ground down and washed out in a continuous process. Between the ball mills is a single-acting rake classifier, another method for selective seperation of the larger and denser particles.
[BB91/25715/PW]

Inside the assay house at Geevor mine in December 1991 where, almost two years after the final closure of the mine, apparatus is still lining the bench, and drawers still contain the crucibles and other equipment. Regular samples from the working-places, and from each stage in the mill, were analysed here. As the tin is not easily visible to the naked eye, the results were crucial in helping to direct and control the everyday working of the mine and the treatment plant.

[BB91/25680/PW]

On the wall racks at Geevor, also in December 1991, were other items that were formerly in everyday use. These included stored samples in packets, circular metal sieves and rectangular wooden-framed ones, along with wooden-handled pans for drying the samples.

[BB91/25681/PW]

In the South Crofty assay laboratory stand a stack of metal trays, battered and
surreal. These are in daily use for heating the ore samples from the mine in an oven
to dry them before the samples are crushed, ground and analysed. [AA000450/PW]

There are few remnants of the tin-streaming works that once flanked the whole course of the Red River near Camborne. The last survivor of the once numerous waterwheels that powered these works is this overshot wheel, formerly fed by the water supply to the long-established corn mill at Reskadinnick. It powered a 'pulveriser' by means of the geared up layshaft that runs out of the left-hand side of the picture. The pulveriser was a rotating drum in which the tin-bearing sediments were tumbled with hard pebbles or scrap iron in order to liberate more of the fine-grained cassiterite. [AA98/03083/PW]

The shroud of the waterwheel of the Reskadinnick Tin-streaming Works was cast by F Bartle and Sons at their Carn Brea foundry between Camborne and Redruth. (This foundry is seen in the illustration on page 136.) Constructed as recently as 1901 the waterwheel has long been out of use. Most of the woodwork has gone and the fractured castings are now very vulnerable. [AA98/03087/PW]

The overshot waterwheel that drives the stamps and the 'buddle' at Blue Hills in Trevellas Coombe, St. Agnes (a buddle is shown in the illustration on page 103). It is the only water-wheel to remain of many that operated in the valley formerly. The flap in the bottom of the launder feeding the wheel is shown open, allowing the water to run to waste. The rope and lever mechanism allows the flap to be closed by remote control, thus starting the wheel. The stamps shown in the illustration on page 106, is on the far side of the stone wall. The original waterwheel was scrapped and this replacement came from a waterworks near Truro that, coincidentally, was situated on a watercourse called the Trevella Stream. [AA98/10290/PW]

The purpose of many of the small waterwheels in tin-streaming works was to lift various tin-bearing slurries to higher levels. Pictured here is a waterwheel at Tolgus Tin-streaming Works near Redruth. Beyond is a dipper wheel, fitted with small offset buckets, that used to empty the lifted load of pulp into a wooden trough that is visible on the far side of the top of the wheel. [AA98/03107/PW]

A small building at Blue Hills, Trevellas Coombe, St. Agnes that was once a burning house. Here the concentrated tin ore was roasted in order to rid it of troublesome sulphide minerals. Its original function is not readily apparent from the outside. [AA98/10288/PW]

Amongst other salvaged items of machinery lying at King Edward Mine near Camborne is a dipper wheel, probably from a local tin-streaming works. It shows the offset buckets clearly. [AA98/10637/PW]

The interior of the same building at Blue Hills shows where the original furnace used to be on the right-hand side, with the flue that formerly ran out to a chimney. The building is still in use and metallic tin is produced in the furnace on the left. [AA98/10289/PW]

Further salvaged items dumped by the King Edward Mine. It is the cast-iron centre for a wooden round frame, such as the one shown in Plate 130. Only two round frames appear to have survived complete in Cornwall. [AA98/10636/PW]

Examples of smelted tin from local ores, concentrated on-site, at Blue Hills. A bar of pure tin will emit a unique whining whisper as it is bent. [AA98/10305/PW]

Concentrated tin ore on a vanning shovel at Blue Hills, Trevellas Coombe, St. Agnes. It is being demonstrated by Mr Wills junior. The cassiterite, or tin oxide, is the brownish tail towards the end of the shovel. The vanning shovel is a traditional tool that has always been used by tin dressers with great dexterity and skill. Around it has developed a mystique that was said to have been passed down from father to son. [AA98/10302/PW]

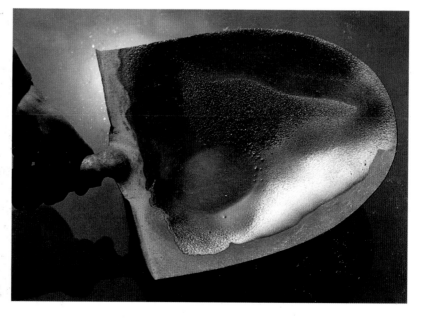

Buildings

This selection of the buildings at, or associated with, tin mines shows something of the wide range of functional types. The older examples are attractive, but the relatively recent ones are more controversial. All these buildings show character.

The traditional mine buildings are of local stone, and it is significant that the ones of granite have been more enduring than those constructed from the altered rocks that occur outside the granite areas. More use was made of timber, both above and below ground, than is apparent now, but much has either been re-used elsewhere or salvaged for fuel. What remained has largely succumbed to the inevitable decay that accompanies the mild, damp climate of the peninsula.

More recent buildings have followed the functional trends of many other types of industrial structure. A limited life span was envisaged and they became very utilitarian in character. Many are of concrete in various forms and in sombre shades of grey, but others are in corrugated iron, displaying a rich variety of colour.

An enduring element in the mining scene is the stone-built terrace housing that characterises the Cornish mining towns and villages. Most still perform their original function, although some of their traditional details are disappearing relentlessly. When local mining was at its peak virtually all these dwellings would have been occupied by families that either worked in the mines, or in trades directly associated with mining.

From the earliest times Cornwall and Devon have seen the complete range of tin-producing processes, but the last phase, the production of the pure metal, was gradually transferred away from this area to take place in northern England and, finally, in Asia. Despite this, two rare surviving examples of traditional tin smelting houses have been included.

An aerial view of Robinson's Shaft at South Crofty looking eastwards. This shows the exceptional compact group of buildings, mostly dating from the first decade of the 20th century. The beam engine house is immediately behind the headframe and the winding engine house is just to the left of it. The air compressors used to be to the left again, with the chimney for their former steam engine. On the nearer side of the yard are the carpenters' and blacksmiths' shops and, some distance over to the left of these, are the remains of the old circular powder house. Curving away to the right, just in front of the powder house is the line of the former tramway that took the ore to the mill for treatment. This tramway used to cross the mine yard, and its line can be followed beyond the yard to the group of buildings at the top of the picture. This particular group was the original South Wheal Crofty, established in the 1850s, with the mine buildings to the left and old shafts to the right. Sadly some of these buildings have been demolished since this photograph was taken in 1998. [NMR 15887-17]

Looking west from Robinson's Shaft at South Crofty showing the distant headframe of Cook's Shaft. Across the yard is the end of the range that contained the blacksmiths' shop. There is some doubt as to whether the Christmas bonus scheme ever received official approval! [BB95/09764/PW]

An electrical sub-station that was built in about 1906. It supplied electricity to the new Californian stamps and ore treatment plant that were being erected near Cook's Shaft at South Crofty. The power was purchased from the company that operated the tramway connecting Camborne and Redruth. The sub-station still fulfils its original function, but with modern equipment. [BB95/09703/PW]

Opposite top: When Robinson's Shaft is viewed from the south-east the functional elegance of the engine house and contemporaneous structures, despite the truncation of the chimneys, contrasts with the unsympathetic modern additions. [BB95/09758/PW]

Opposite below: The current blacksmiths' shop at South Crofty probably dates from about 1920 and occupies a corner of the Bartle's Foundry site close to Cook's Shaft. In the background can be seen the two internal forges, a pair of anvils and, against the right-hand wall, racks of tools. (For a close up of these tools *see* the illustration on page 167). In the foreground is a pneumatic hammer by Alldays and Onions, probably of about the same date as the building. This delivers a hammer blow equivalent to 3 hundredweights. [BB95/09717/PW]

A foundry alongside Cook's Shaft at South Crofty that was
established to supply castings for the mining industry. It is a
rare survivor of the small foundries that were vital to tin
mining and processing. [AA98/03088/PW]

Opposite top: An impressive double-pile storage shed of corrugated iron on a timber frame. It stands south-
east of Cook's Shaft at South Crofty although it was originally associated with the foundry in the illustration
above. Bartle's Foundry to the east. [BB95/9701/PW]

Opposite below: One of two cast-iron lintels of the smithy of Wheal Busy, near Chacewater. The impressive
building contained, in addition to the smithy, a fitting shop, offices and a miners' dry. The lintels were cast at
Perran Foundry and appear to have been inserted into an older building at a time of short-lived expansion.
The long-established tin and copper mine closed in 1873, with some later working for arsenic being carried
out from 1907 until 1924. Wheal Busy is famous for its series of early historic steam-pumping engines.
[AA98/10312/PW]

The calciner that was used for roasting the ore at the old Botallack Mine, St. Just in Penwith, prior to the building of the structure shown in the illustration *below*. The hot gases passed along a rubble flue to the right of the building leading to a chimney. The headframe in the distance was erected by the management of Geevor Mine over Allen's Shaft in the 1980s to investigate the potential of this area. The chimney nearby remains from the original sinking of this shaft in 1908. This headframe and chimney are also shown on page 53. [AA98/10383/PW]

The arsenic labyrinth and stack at Allen's Shaft, Botallack. Arsenic, once of little value, had become a significant by-product of some of the tin and copper mines from the 1870s onwards. This new labyrinth was constructed in the first decade of the 20th century although the chimney is older, having served an earlier beam-engine house. The arch was to carry the flues over the mine tramway. [AA98/10384/PW]

Above: A Brunton calciner at Tolgus near Redruth. The concentrated tin ore was roasted on a rotating bed in this building in order to burn off some of the impurities. The shed on the right offered some protection from the weather for the fuel and the stoker. The hot gases passed through a flue that runs up the hillside to the chimney on the skyline. Noxious elements were discharged from the stack – hence its location on the south-western side of the valley, so that the fumes could be better dispersed by the prevailing wind, but arsenic was salvaged from the flues. This whole group of structures is protected as a 'listed' building. [AA98/03106/PW]

Right: An eye-catching and functional mine building north of Cook's Shaft at South Crofty. [AA000412/PW]

One of the 1960s sheds at Wheal Jane that was erected as
part of the exploration phase that preceded the sinking of the
shafts. Only after the tin-treatment plant was built did it
become a 'dangerous substances store'. [AA98/10493/PW]

Not all relatively
modern mine
buildings are
purely functional
and devoid of
artistic merit, as
is shown by this
pleasantly
detailed exten-
sion near Victory
Shaft at Geevor.
[BB92/14645/PW]

A humble building at King Edward Mine, near Camborne, that is full of character and probably dates from the 1890s. Originally it comprised the mine assay office and weighbridge office and it is now a grade II* 'listed' building in its own right. [AA98/10638/PW]

Another view of surface facilities at the King Edward Mine. In the centre is the blacksmith's shop, with the toilet to the left. In the left-hand foreground is the corner of the survey office. In the right-hand foreground is the mill, with the workshop beyond it and, in the background, the miners' dry. The assay office and weighbridge office range seen in the illustration *above* is in the left-hand distance. [AA98/10639/PW]

Left: Virtually the only surviving trace of Wheal Clifford at St. Day is this delightful powder house on United Downs. It is a rare survival of the kind of building that was once relatively common in mining areas. [AA98/08966/PW]

Below: Detail of the top of the circular wall surrounding an abandoned explosives magazine near Robinson's Shaft at South Crofty. It probably dates from the 1850s and can be seen towards the bottom left-hand corner of the illustration on page 132, just above the curve of the former tramway. The broken bottles constitute a colourful deterrent. [AA000485/PW]

Count houses were effectively the offices of the mines. They show great variation in size and pretension that bore little relation to the mine's prosperity. This small example is the count house of Carnelloe Mine, Zennor, and is now a private house. [AA98/09001/JOD]

The count house of Botallack Mine near St. Just in Penwith is one of the grander examples. It is shown after the completion of a recent extensive restoration programme by The National Trust. [AA99/04956/PW]

The Mining Exchange at
Redruth. A late 19th-century
'listed' building incorporating
a ticketing office, it is thought
to be by the local architect
Sampson Hill. [AA98/03104/PW]

Of much more recent date, the
Men's Institute at Pendeen, St.
Just in Penwith appears as a
purely functional building. Now
reroofed, and with windows
blocked, its destiny seems to have
mirrored the fortune of the local
tin industry. [AA98/10257/PW]

In the late 19th and early 20th centuries there appeared a series of workers' institutes in the mining areas, particularly in west Cornwall. They range widely in scale and design, but all have character. This fine example is the 1893 Miners and Mechanics' Institute, St Agnes, in Vicarage Road at St. Agnes. It is one of four institutes in Cornwall donated by J Passmore Edwards, and is to a design by W J Wills. [BB98/13683/PW]

The Pool Basset Institute near Redruth dates from 1878. Its foundation stone was laid by Arthur Francis Basset of Tehidy. (Tehidy was the Basset family home north of Camborne.) The architecture is perhaps a precursor of the buildings associated with Marriott's Shaft of the Basset group of mines, not very far away, that were erected in about 1900. [AA009028/JOD]

The hamlet of Carnkie, near Redruth, suddenly became a focal point when a number of ailing local mines were constituted into the eastern section of the Basset Mines in the early 1890s. The hamlet grew rapidly, but suffered a severe setback in 1918 with the closure of the mines. The Carnkie Men's Institute appears not to have been built until 1924. The architecture is original, but backward-looking, and does not have the bold corporate style of the previous example. [AA98/10404/PW]

A tiny building beside the road at Penhellick Institute, Carn Brea, that has long been reduced to use as a garage. Despite its small size it carries the proud inscription 'INSTITUTE' in relief. It was for the benefit of local miners in a concentrated mining area and probably dates from the beginning of the 20th century. [AA98/16741/PW]

A late 19th-century miners' terrace at Tuckingmill, near Camborne, that is characteristic of the area. Well-built, with individual walled front gardens, the range of buildings has a pleasing unity. The aesthetic appeal of these terraces is being eroded with the camouflaging of attractive local stone and the ripping out of distinguished horned sash windows. With the cessation of mining activities upstream the Red River in the foreground runs clear for the first time in many hundreds of years. [BB97/03976/PW]

Some Camborne streets were constructed as a single terraced development. Many, as seen here in Union Street, consist of houses that conform generally, and present a unified building line, although they are individual structures and present subtle architectural and decorative differences. [AA98/16735/PW]

56 Union Street, Camborne. An example of the architectural detail that
gives a humble member of a terrace an air of distinction. The differences
in window heights and sizes, roof-lines and floor levels all indicate the
individuality of design of many of these dwellings. [AA98/16738/PW]

Unsympathetic replacement of original doors and windows has eroded the integrity of streets such as Tolcarne Street, Camborne, but the well-built houses continue to be in demand. As in the previous photographs, most of the families who lived here originally would have depended on the mining industry for their livelihood. [AA98/16736/PW]

An attractive pair of early 19th-century cottages almost opposite the main gate of South Crofty. These dwellings would have been associated with mining in some way, as there were contemporaneous mines all around. The immediate surroundings would have been rural, however, and the impact of the huge installation of stamps and other heavy machinery at Cook's Shaft and the adjoining treatment plant, only a short distance to the west, must have been devastating (*see* the illustration on page 182). [AA98/03093/PW]

Opposite top: The Treloweth smelting house at St. Erth is one of the very few tin smelters to have survived in south-west England. Now more usually known as the Lamb and Flag tin smelter, it was erected in 1715, was rebuilt in 1825, and closed in 1883. This photograph shows how much character still remains. The roof timbers are smoke-blackened and, along the top of the arcade wall, still lies a thick deposit of black soot from the furnaces. The 'Lamb and Flag' persists as the sign for the adjacent public house, shown in the illustration on page 172, and an ingot of tin from this smelter is shown in the illustration on page 174. [AA99/05028/PW]

Opposite below: Another tin smelter that has survived is the Union Tin-smelting Works near Weir Quay at Bere Ferrers, Devon. This shows the main entrance to the smelter building, fronted by a small yard and protected by massive granite gateposts. There are also a count house and an assay office. The buildings probably date from 1849 and they were in use until about 1890. [AA99/04985/PW]

Chapel and Graveyard

Cornwall was visited by Celtic missionaries from Ireland and Wales and many of their names have survived as those of saints. St. Piran came here in the 6th century and became the patron saint of tin miners but, somewhat like the industry he represented, a chapel dedicated to him is now buried deep in the sand dunes near Perranporth.

The only English cathedral west of Exeter is at Truro, built between 1880 and about 1910, and it is fitting that a romanticised mining scene should be included in its stained glass. The windswept parish church of the tin-bearing area is, in contrast, generally a low building of granite or slate, with a robust plain tower. There is not the opulence, nor even the ornamentation, seen in other parts of the country. Instead, there is an aesthetic solidity with a textural focus.

Methodism had been introduced to St. Ives in 1743. It spread quickly and many societies were formed. In marked contrast to Devon the numerous, stone Methodist chapels are prominent features in the Cornish landscape. Indeed, it is only in Wales that the boldness and frequency of the chapel exceeds that in Cornwall. Many of those in the tin-mining area feature in the RCHME volume by Christopher Stell on the *Chapels and Meeting-houses in South-West England* (HMSO 1991).

Graveyards give an indication of the personal tragedies that accompanied tin mining in Cornwall. Some examples have been selected from those that show a connection with the industry. How many more must there be to men, women and children whose death was as a direct result of mining, but whose brief commemorative lines make no mention of the fact?

The gravestone of 25-year-old Vingoe Trembath in Pendeen churchyard is a sad reminder of the one Cornish tin-mining accident that is widely known outside the county. Levant had the last surviving man-engine in the country. Powered by a steam engine, this was for raising and lowering miners on platforms attached to a near vertical rod that was moving up and down between a series of platforms that were fixed. By stepping from one to the other at the top or bottom of each stroke, the men moved upwards or downwards. On 20 October 1919 the connection at the top of the contrivance broke when it was bringing miners back to the surface, and thirty-one men lost their lives. [AA98/03161/PW]

A reconstruction by John Scott Martin of the scene at Levant on that fateful day in 1919. Families and friends, desperate for news, cluster around the count house. In the foreground, close to the shaft containing the man-engine, are gathered men who were involved in the working of the mine. Each group appears stunned, incapable of taking in the scale of the tragedy, powerless to help. Smoke comes from the whim chimney suggesting that this may have been in use to provide emergency access via Skip Shaft, seen immediately to the left, to the scenes of carnage below. To the right of the whim house is the engine house containing a 45-inch Cornish pumping engine with its boiler house and stack on the right. In the distance, to the right again, is the Cornish stamps engine house. On the left-hand side of the picture is the chimney of the calciner. (The illustration on page 33 is a recent view of Skip Shaft with the engine houses for the whim and pump.)

[© John Scott Martin]

CORNISH·MINERS·WORKING·AT·DOLCOATH

Part of a stained glass window donated by the Tregoning family at the west end of Truro Cathedral showing Cornish miners working at Dolcoath, one of the greatest of the Cornish mines. The scene is romanticised, dating from some time around the turn of the last century. Three men and a boy are seen labouring below a mine headframe and beside a shaft. In the background is Carn Brea with an attenuated Basset Monument on the skyline. The window was made by the London firm of Clayton and Bell, founded in 1850 by two assistants in Gilbert Scott's office. Another window in the cathedral shows John Wesley preaching in Gwennap Pit (*see* the illusration *below*). [BB98/11580/MHR]

Gwennap Pit at Busveal, St. Day, is an atmospheric open-air venue where John Wesley first preached in 1762. Altogether he preached here seventeen times, the last being in 1789, only about a year before his death. Gwennap Pit is in a concentrated mining area and it has been suggested that the pit was originally the result of mining subsidence. The ready acceptance of the pit for public gatherings and the lack of later ground movement throw some doubt on this suggestion, however. The pit was reconstructed as a memorial to John Wesley in 1806–7. [AA98/10218/PW]

A charming slate memorial fixed inside the church at Zennor records the death of Matthew Thomas aged 44, in August 1809. Wheal Chance was a small tin mine that once existed south of the village but, like any explanation of the fatal 'fall of ground', it has long gone. [AA98/03149/JOD]

Below; Left: Sancreed is a Penwith parish that once contained various small tin mines, as is recorded in one of the panels of the east window of the church dedicated to Saint Sancredus. The window commemorates Thomas Bedford Bolitho (1835—1915) and Frances Jane Bolitho (1864—1936). This panel includes a stylised mine tunnel below a landscape containing a headframe and an engine house. Within the mine is shown a miner, down on one knee, with a hand-axe in his right hand and his 'croust', or lunch, tied in a handkerchief. Illumination is provided by a burning candle stuck onto the front of his helmet, and unused candles hang against his chest. [AA009029/JOD]

Right: In Calstock churchyard are various tombstones that testify to the dangers of mining and the tragic price that parishioners and itinerant workers paid for their working in the local mines. One gravestone commemorating a mine accident is the one to John Pascoe who was killed in 'Drake Walls Mine' in February 1850, aged 34, unfortunately there is no information about how the accident occurred. Drakewalls is an old mine just south of Gunnislake. [AA98/08621/PW]

In the graveyard of the parish church at St. Just in Penwith, careful parting of the vegetation reveals the depth of tragedy in one local mining family. Not only was John Victor killed in Botallack Mine in June 1852, aged 22, but he had been deprived of his father, Howard, who had lost his life after an accident in Boscaswell Mine, aged 48, twenty years earlier. [AA98/08968/JOD]

Perhaps the most tragic of the gravestones at Calstock is the one to Isaac Sleep, a 14-year-old 'who was accidentally kill'd in Virtuous-Lady-Mine by the crank of the water wheel' in August 1831. This old mine was near Buckland Monachorum in Devon and was mainly for copper. The reference to the waterwheel's crank suggests that it was driving a drainage pump at the mine. It is not made clear if the boy was an employee of the mine at the time of the accident. [AA98/08622/PW]

The Methodist church built at Carnkie, a tin-mining settlement near Redruth, in 1904–5 when the Basset Mines nearby were at their peak. The proximity of the mining can be seen by the pair of chimneys to the left. Prosperity in the area was short-lived as these tin mines closed in 1918. [AA98/10216/PW]

THIS STONE
IS ERECTED IN
SAD REMEMBRANCE OF
three Children Sons of
WILLIAM & ANN WALTER,
LATE OF DEVONSHIRE,
whose deaths were caused
by an explosion of Gunpowder,
WHILST AT PLAY AT DOLCOATH
on June 20th,
1868,
Names and Ages
JAMES OLIVER 9 Years
AUGUSTAS Years
ALFRED LEWIS 5 Years
ALSO OF

A dreadful illustration of the danger to children in the tin-mining environment is shown by this gravestone in Camborne churchyard in memory of four boys, aged between 5 and 9, who were killed by an explosion that they had created when playing with matches at a powder house at Dolcoath Mine. Three of the boys came from a single family. At the inquest a verdict of accidental death was recorded. It did result in some safety improvements being made, but too late for the Walter family who, at a stroke, had lost three out of eight children. [AA98/08624/JOD]

There remain an eclectic series of images that have a direct association with tin and that illustrate the wide effect that the industry has had. Included are such varied aspects as transport, tools and equipment, underground headgear and lighting, rock samples from the exploration phase of mining, surveying instruments, the depiction of tin-mining scenes in art, 'pub' signs, and the marks on tin ingots. Some of the images stray into the subject areas dealt with in the other chapters. Here is an opportunity to broaden the appreciation of what is thought relevant to the subject of tin and to consider some of the interaction that has taken place between industry and art.

In the tin mines of Cornwall and Devon women and girls did not work underground but they did carry out various surface tasks as 'bal maidens', particularly on the floors where the ore was dressed for treatment. This illustration is from *Half Hours Underground*, published in 1888 in the anonymous *Half Hour Library* series. Although this maiden appears in the section on the tin mines of the St. Just district the shape of the shovel that she holds is not one that is seen generally in Cornwall. In the distance can be seen a most fanciful representation of a headframe over a shaft, and there is a train hauled by a steam engine – a rare sight indeed as the main line never extended further west than Penzance!

Right: A turntable in the yard beside Robinson's Shaft at South Crofty. It enabled a load to be drawn from any of three directions to go down in the cage. Similarly a wagon or electric locomotive from underground could be rotated and guided onto the selected track. Unusually, South Crofty operated with a 22-inch gauge track. [BB95/09762/PW]

Below: A warning board, now preserved at the Tolgus Tin Museum, near Redruth. It is clearly an official railway sign and includes the convention of 'up', referring to trains travelling in the direction of London, rather than referring to any gradient on the line. On a number of lines the mines were an important source of revenue for the railway company and a few branches were virtually restricted to mine traffic. [AA98/03110/PW]

ALL UP MINERAL TRAINS To STOP DEAD HERE

A version of a miner's hat that appeared as another illustration in the tin-mining section of the 1888 publication *Half Hours Underground*. Neither this style of lamp, nor its method of attachment seems to have caught on in south-west England where the candle, stuck to the hat with a lump of clay, was standard practice. Eventually the acetylene lamp appeared, as seen in the illustration on page 164, followed by the now universal electric version with a belt-secured rechargeable battery.

Miners required headgear that would cushion the head from the rock, deflect small pieces that might fall from the roof and support a clay-held candle to provide light. Before the introduction of modern 'hard hats' miners often wore helmets made of felt, strengthened with resin. Shown here are two such examples that were found in an abandoned workplace in South Crofty in the 1960s.

[A S collection, AA95/02792/JOD]

A small commemorative figure of a Cornish miner standing on a lump of rich tin ore at Menabilly House, near Fowey. This outstanding country house is the home of the Rashleigh family, well-known in the world of mining and minerals. The inscription records that the piece was 'Presented to the Officers of the Royal Miners by their last Honorary Colonel Sir Colman B. Rashleigh, Bart. in remembrance of his Command of the Regt. 1892–96'. It is interesting to speculate how many other tin-related objects may exist in the homes of traditional Cornish families. [BB001427/PW]

A Staffordshire dish at the Royal Institution of Cornwall in Truro produced specifically for Boscean Mine, a tin mine half a mile north-west of St. Just in Penwith. The dish dates from 1854, a period of brief prosperity for the mine which became part of Cunning United in 1871, and seems to have closed finally in, or about, 1877. [BB98/13698/PW]

The plinth of Richard Trevithick's statue in Camborne (*see* page 164) carries interesting bronze panels. The one showing a Cornish boiler is the work of L. S. Merrifield in 1919, having been cast by A. B. Burton. Such boilers performed a crucial function in producing relatively high-pressure steam for mining and other machinery. Two examples are seen on pages 61 and 62. [AA98/03148/PW]

THE ADVENTURERS IN.
HALLENBEAGLE.MINE.
1839

Detail of the Levant Mine long-case clock dating from 1830, a period of great prosperity for the mine. This is at the Royal Institution of Cornwall in Truro. The painted mining scene in the arch above the dial shows a certain lack of technical authenticity. Some fanciful architectural elements and the depiction of a circular shaft collar have more in common with Midland collieries than with this Cornish tin and copper mine, and it is significant that the clock was manufactured in Birmingham. [BB98/13702/PW]

Opposite page: A very attractive example of a Swansea punch jug at the Royal Institution of Cornwall in Truro. It was produced for Hallenbeagle Mine at Scorrier, near Redruth, and comes from the mine's most profitable period when it employed nearly 200 people. At the site the pair of ruined engine houses can still be seen close to the railway and main road. Hallenbeagle Mine was primarily known for copper but later it became part of the tin and copper mine of Great Wheal Busy. [BB98/13699/PW]

Another Swansea punch jug, also at the Royal Institution of Cornwall in Truro. It bears the name of Francis Pryor, a Cornishman who lived from 1819 to 1870. He worked in North Roskear mine , East Pool and Tolcarne Mines in the Camborne district and is reputed to have made his fortune, although most of this went on drink. The jug shows a rotative beam engine winding from a shaft, and the depiction of an external boiler is of interest. The diminutive size of the engine house, and one or two other details, appear more in keeping with coal mining in South Wales. [BB98/13700/PW]

'St. Just Tin Miners' is also at the Royal Institution of Cornwall in Truro. It was painted in 1935 by Harold Harvey (1874–1941) and is presumably based on Geevor Mine. The miners have acetylene lamps on their helmets: the method of illumination whilst working underground which was used after the traditional candle and before the appearance of the modern battery-powered electric lamp.

[St. Just Tin Miners, 1935 by Harold Harvey (1874–1941) The Royal Institution of Cornwall, Truro, Cornwall, UK/Bridgeman Art Library]

Much of Richard Trevithick's work was associated with mining, and the high-pressure steam engine that he invented became the workhorse for exploiting the deep Cornish tin deposits. Long after his death, a bronze statue was erected to commemorate Camborne's most celebrated inhabitant. This statue stands at a focal point in the town, outside the Passmore Edwards Free Library at the bottom of Camborne Hill, and it shows him holding a locomotive and a pair of dividers. A panel from the plinth of this statue is shown on page 161. [AA98/08956/PW]

Another delightful oil painting at the Royal Institution of Cornwall in Truro is by the Cornish artist John Opie (1761–1807) and is entitled 'A gentleman and a miner with a specimen of copper ore'. The gentleman is Thomas Daniel of Truro (1715–93) and the miner is Captain Morcom of St. Agnes, who is in typical clothing including a skullcap, over which while working he would most likely have worn a protective hat. In the background is a pumping beam engine at work and, to the left of it, a capstan for hoisting in the shaft, probably horse-powered. This painting was exhibited in the Royal Academy in 1786 and the depiction of an early engine house is of some interest. The engine is likely to have been built by Boulton and Watt in Birmingham. Although their first beam engine in Cornwall had started work only in 1777, by the end of 1786 the number of their engines working in the County had risen to an amazing total of 36. It is thought that the scene may have been of Polberro Mine, a well-known tin and copper mine at St. Agnes.

[A gentleman and a miner with a specimen of copper ore by John Orie (1761–1807)
The Royal Institution of Cornwall, Truro, Cornwall, UK/Bridgeman Art Library]

A striking portrait in oils of Captain Charles Thomas, painted by William Cock in 1866, now hanging in the Royal Institution of Cornwall in Truro. Captain Thomas (1794–1868) was a staunch Methodist and the manager of Dolcoath, and other mines, from 1844 until his death. He is shown reading *The Mining Journal* for September 1866. [BB98/13697/PW]

A detail of the cast-iron base of the drill sharpener that stands in the blacksmiths' shop at Robinson's Shaft, South Crofty. Made locally, this machine was for sharpening the removable underground drill bits that the miners used for drilling into the rock. Regular and accurate grinding on this sharpener maintained the cutting power of the bits and extended their life.
[AA000488/PW]

Blacksmiths' tools on racks in the forge at Cook's Shaft of South Crofty. It might be thought that the white coating was to enable the tools to be located amongst the coal, ash and dust. In fact, when the internal walls were sprayed white, the tools were not removed first.
[AA000478/PW]

Such a rack, full of spare pipe connections, parts of pumps, screens and washers, was once a vital element in maintaining the smooth operation of the treatment plant at Wheal Jane. Although they create an atmospheric scene, the individual items now have very little value.
[AA98/10462/MHR]

A pile of abandoned drill-core is now the only
tangible evidence of the long and expensive
exploration phase that preceded the sinking of the
shafts for extraction of tin ore at Wheal Jane.
Thousands of feet of such cores were produced by
diesel-powered rigs that drilled with diamond-
studded bits to produce a continuous rock sample
over the length of each borehole. [AA98/10480/PW]

Abandoned mineralised samples in a shed at Wheal Jane. Such samples were taken from drill-core and from initial underground development. Generally each was crushed and split into two portions. One was analysed for tin and other metals, and the other was retained for reference. In this case the samples have outlived the life of the mine for which they were the precursor. [AA98/10491/PW]

In the museum at Geevor Mine, St. Just, is a fine instrument still in its original wooden case by William Wilton of St. Day, a mathematical instrument maker. It is a sophisticated version of the miners' dial, the traditional instrument for surveying underground workings. It has telescopic sights instead of the more usual cross-hairs and, using a combination of the graduated semicircle, the telescope and the relevant bubble-level, it could be used for surveying inclined shafts and raises, enabling the line of sight to be related to a horizontal bearing. [BB98/13706/PW]

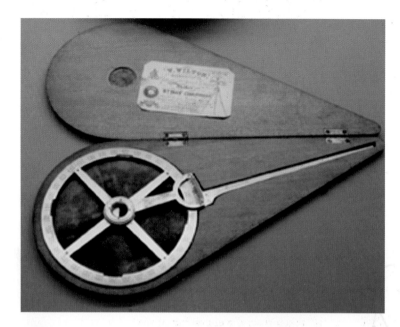

Another example of the work of William Wilton, again in its original case, is to be found at the Royal Institution of Cornwall in Truro. It is an instrument for plotting the results of sightings that had been taken with a miners' dial such as the one in the previous illustration. The arm enables the line of sight to be ruled to the correct bearing and a Vernier scale, for increased accuracy, is visible at the interface between the arm and the graduated circle. [BB98/13703/PW]

A 'listed' building behind Church Street in St. Day is a remarkable survival. It is thought to date from the 1840s and was the workshop of William Wilton. In all probability both the surveying instruments that are shown were made here. William Wilton used this workshop until 1876 when he emigrated to Valparaiso. [AA99/03042/PW]

Mining communities and the keeping of pigeons often go together. The vehicle in the mine car park at South Crofty shows that Cornish miners were no exception in their spare-time interest. Perhaps the appeal came from the freedom of flight that was such a contrast to the men's other life underground. [AA000414/PW]

Many inn signs in Cornwall illustrate aspects of the tin-mining industry. The 'Miners Arms' at Mithian, near St. Agnes, shows a romanticised engine house on the cliffs, presumably loosely based on one of those at nearby St. Agnes. [AA98/03103/PW]

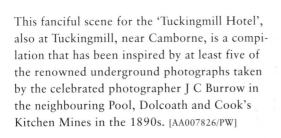

The 'Pendarves Arms' at Tuckingmill, near Camborne, portrays a surface scene at the nearby tin and copper mine of Dolcoath. It is clearly taken from the engraving of the illustration on page 14, but the naïve added effects belie the fact that Dolcoath was the greatest of the tin mines until it closed in 1920. The Pendarves family were local land and mineral owners who profited greatly from this and other local tin mines. [AA98/03100/JOD]

This fanciful scene for the 'Tuckingmill Hotel', also at Tuckingmill, near Camborne, is a compilation that has been inspired by at least five of the renowned underground photographs taken by the celebrated photographer J C Burrow in the neighbouring Pool, Dolcoath and Cook's Kitchen Mines in the 1890s. [AA007826/PW]

The device of a lamb with St. George's flag had become a symbol of England long before the adoption of the Union Flag. It is thought to have had its origin in the wool trade that had been so important to the country's economy in medieval times. Henry Davies, at the Treloweth smelter at St. Erth in 1715 (*see* the illustration on page 151), was the first to use the mark of a lamb and flag on blocks of tin and it soon became a standard mark for the produce of Cornish smelters (examples are seen in the illustration on page 174). The Treloweth smelter was later owned by the Daubuz family but it closed in 1883. This sign at St. Erth is outside the public house which stands beside the Treloweth, or 'Lamb and Flag' smelting house. [AA95/04982/PW]

Another example of a sign with a mining theme is seen at the 'Rambling Miner' at Chacewater, near Truro. Here the miner has a needle-sharp pick, a bunch of candles over his shoulder, and even a clay-mounted candle on the front of his hat. The map of the world in the background is a reminder of the difficult times in tin mining in Cornwall, particularly in the last quarter of the 19th century, that forced many miners to emigrate to distant mining fields. [AA98/03102/PW]

Surely the limits of artistic licence have been reached at the 'Miners Arms' at St. Just in Penwith. That the one-armed gentleman is a local tin miner is made clear in the Cornish language (The tin workers' alehouse), but why the wink or the jaunty rake of the clay-mounted candle? Through the window behind him can be seen what can only be assumed to be an engine house with a smoking chimney. [AA98/03101/PW]

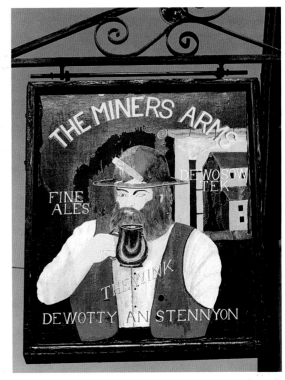

A model of an underground area of working in the first decade of the 20th century on display in the museum at Geevor Mine. This shows the different ways in which the ponderous compressed-air drills used to be set up before the 'air-leg' (see the illustration on page 90, and the front cover) came into general use. [BB98/13705/PW]

found it being used as a
house.

At the Royal Institution of Cornwall in Truro is an extensive collection of the marks that decorated the blocks of tin cast at the Cornish smelting houses. Two of the marks are from the Redruth Tin Smelting Company which started production in 1862, was relaunched under limited liability in 1887, and was the last tin smelter to close in Cornwall, in 1923. The Bolitho family was associated with five tin smelters in the county and the one at the top is probably from the Chyandour smelting house, at Penzance, that closed in 1912. The mark at the bottom left is from the Calenick smelter, near Truro, that closed in 1891. [BB98/13695/PW]

Three of five tin ingots in the Royal Institution of Cornwall collection in Truro. They came from the cargo of the *SS Cheerful* that sank after a collision on 20 July 1885. The ingots were salvaged in 1994 from a point 18 miles (29 km) off St. Ives at a depth of over 200 feet (61 m). The three ingots shown all carry the lamb and flag mark, which by this time had come to be generally accepted as a sign of purity of the tin. Two of them, one of 28 lbs (12.7 kg) and one of 56 lbs (25.4 kg), had come from the Carvedras smelter in Truro. The middle one of 56 lbs (25.4 kg) came from Treloweth at St. Erth, where the lamb and flag device had first been used as a tin mark. [BB98/13696/PW]

The Final Chapter

In terms of the number of operating tin mines in Cornwall and Devon, the industry has been in decline since the early 1870s. Within months of the final closure of Geevor in 1990 only South Crofty remained at work. This was the last tin mine in Europe to remain in operation, kept going through a combination of cost-cutting efficiency and the indefatigable spirit and personal sacrifices of the men who worked there. The closure of South Crofty in 1998 brought the many centuries of tin mining in Cornwall to an end.

In the present economic climate it is unrealistic to anticipate a sudden increased demand for tin, although there is always the possibility that an unexpected new use for the metal could develop. There are reserves of tin in Cornwall and Devon that could be realised if the price of tin were to rise dramatically. For many centuries this corner of the British Isles has been renowned throughout the world for its tin industry. It is ironic that this very area now has the highest dependence on tourism, so that the environmental constraints on any proposed new mining development here, if permitted, would indeed be onerous and consequently extremely expensive.

A view inside the miners' dry at Geevor, photographed nearly a year after the closure of the mine had prompted the inscription on the locker. [BB91/25688/PW]

The bruised landscape at Wheal Jane after the mine had closed and many of the surface facilities had been removed. In the foreground are the concrete footings that, until recently, had supported the backstays of the headframe of Clemow's Shaft. The site of the capped shaft is marked by the paling fence. In the background can be seen the crusher house, fine-ore conveyor and, in the distance, the overland ore conveyor and the treatment plant. Although the mine had closed in 1991 these facilities remained in use treating the South Crofty ore. [AA98/10508/PW]

Opposite page: Inside the Robinson's mine dry at South Crofty. Although the building has been abandoned, lockers still contain safety boots, a waterproof and some personal items. [BB95/9746/PW]

The clouds of mist billowing from the area by the Cook's Shaft
compressor house on cold or wet days was a visual sign of underground activity. Here, in the closing days of the mine, the mist forms
a backdrop to a growing pile of scrap iron and steel. [AA000528/PW]

Opposite top: One of the sheave wheels from the headframe is all that remains above ground of Clemow's
Shaft at Wheal Jane. Behind it are piles of ore that have been trucked from South Crofty for treatment at the
Wheal Jane mill. The ore will be crushed in the crusher house to the left, from which it will emerge by the
fine-ore conveyor to the right. After this it passes up the long covered conveyor to the mill visible on the
horizon. [AA98/10483/PW]

Opposite below: Two sheave wheels lying in the yard to the south of Cook's Shaft at South Crofty. They have
come from a headframe, presumably a local one. Whether they will ever be used again is doubtful; the best
fate that either can expect now is to become a roadside feature. [AA000411/PW]

A sea of wheels lying on pallets near Cook's Shaft, the result of underground wagons being brought to the surface and stripped down at the end of the mine's life. [AA000413/PW]

Opposite page: Part of a shift waiting to go underground at Cook's Shaft in the final weeks of South Crofty. There is a hint here of the spirit that kept the operation going for so long and that prevailed until the very end. [AA000458/PW]

A view of Cook's
Shaft as it finally
came to rest, seen
from a window
of the abandoned
pair of cottages
nearby shown in
the illustration
on page 150.
[AA98/03096/PW]

On Saturday, 7 March 1998, the day after the closure of South Crofty, a parade marched from Camborne to the mine to celebrate the great tradition of Cornish mining. Here, the procession has just reached Tuckingmill. On the hard-hat of the miner in the foreground is mounted an acetylene lamp (as seen in the illustration on page 164). [A98/17953/JOD]

As can be seen in the reflection in the tuba, the
procession is just reaching its final destination
at South Crofty Mine. [AA98/17967/JOD]

Right: The parade is now over, and Cook's Shaft is framed in Cornish flags. Unlike some other industries in crisis, the miners at South Crofty had taken the news of the forthcoming closure philosophically and, before the mine gates closed for the last time, many had already committed themselves to alternative jobs that would have little in common with their former way of life. [AA009618/JOD]

Below: An illustration of how exploitation in Cornwall has changed. The once functional dipper wheel to the left has become little more than a quaint feature aimed at visitors to the adjacent shop in an attempt to persuade them to include a tin-treatment plant in their excursion. Like Tolgus Tin-streaming Works, how many historic industrial sites will be forced into such an uneasy liaison with the tourist market in order to survive? [AA98/03131/JOD]

The ruins of the mine buildings around Marriott's Shaft of the Basset Mines, near Camborne now have the air of a medieval cloister. The boiler house is shown, with the pumping engine house in the background. (An overall view of the complex is seen on page 31). The masonry has been stabilised, fallen debris removed, the ground levelled and cleared, and pale, sterile gravel introduced. The future of the buildings has been assured but, in satisfying the interests of health and safety, there has been a compromise. As happens so often, the loss has been of that indefinable, but precious, quality of the atmosphere of the site. [AA009628/PW]

A roadside feature at Pendeen, near St. Just in Penwith. How long will it be before this is the image in every child's mind of a typical Cornish tin miner?
[AA98/08948/PW]

Swaledale, its Mines and Smelt Mills
ISBN: 1 84306 018 3   £19.95

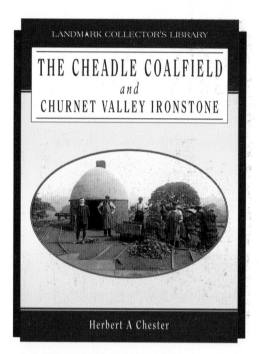

The Cheadle Coalfield
ISBN: 1 84306 013 2   £24.95

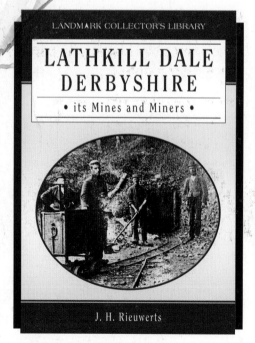

Lathkill Dale, Derbyshire,
its Mines & Miners
ISBN: 1 901522 80 6   £16.95

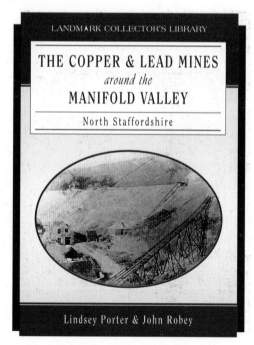

The Copper & Lead Mines around the
Manifold Valley, North Staffordshire
ISBN: 1 901522 77 6   £19.95

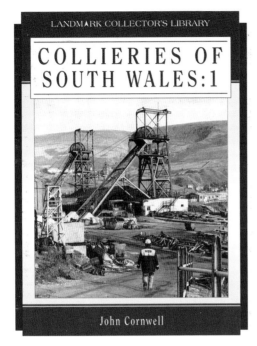

Collieries of South Wales: 1
ISBN: 1 84306 015 9 £22.50

Collieries of Somerset & Bristol
ISBN: 1 84306 029 9 £14.95

Coming soon:
Collieries of South Wales: 2
ISBN: 1 84306 017 5 *(Available Spring 2002)*
Full details upon request

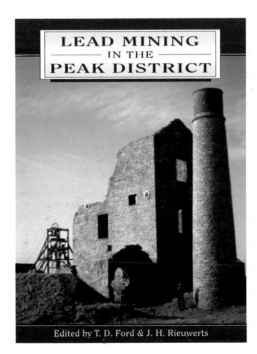

Lead Mining in the Peak District
ISBN: 1 901522 15 6 £9.95